D1325850

The Joy of Cats

Also by Celia Haddon

One Hundred Ways to a Happy Cat
One Hundred Ways for a Cat to Train Its Human
One Hundred Ways for a Cat to Find Its Inner Kitten
One Hundred Secret Thoughts Cats Have About Humans

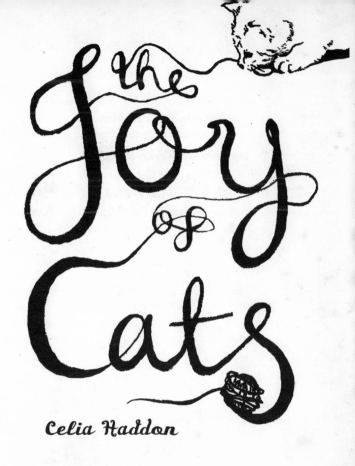

the Joy of Cats

Celia Haddon

HODDER &
STOUGHTON

First published in Great Britain in 2008 by Hodder & Stoughton
An Hachette Livre UK company

1

Copyright © Celia Haddon 2008 in the arrangement
Illustrations © Clare Deasy 2008

The right of Celia Haddon to be identified as the Author
of the Work has been asserted by her in accordance
with the Copyright, Designs and Patents Act 1988.

A CIP catalogue record for this title is available from the British Library

ISBN 978 0340 95459 1

Typeset in Times by Hewer Text UK Ltd, Edinburgh

Printed and bound by Clays Ltd, St Ives plc

Hodder & Stoughton policy is to use papers that are natural,
renewable and recyclable products and made from wood grown in
sustainable forests. The logging and manufacturing processes are expected
to conform to the environmental regulations of the country of origin.

Hodder & Stoughton Ltd
338 Euston Road
London NW1 3BH

www.hodder.co.uk

*In memory of George, most playful of black cats,
who vanished on October 28th 2007.*

Contents

Introduction

Cats have padded silently into our hearts, bringing with them their grace, their independence and their essential mystery. How have we humans become so fond of these small desert creatures with their sharp claws and carnivorous teeth? Why do we love them so much?

Dogs may be humans' best friends, willing to work obediently for us, anxious to please us, and always looking up to us. Cats don't do that kind of friendship. As the saying goes, 'Dogs look up to us; cats look down on us.' They give us the pleasure of their company but never their obedience. If your cat does what you want him to do, that's only because he wants to do it anyway.

It's the free spirit in cats that attracts most of us, I think. Women who love cats too much, of which I am one, actually delight in the way our cats never quite give all of themselves. Like a tantalising love affair, we are never quite sure of the loved one. Yes, he loves us – but how much? Emotionally, as well as literally, cats elude our grasp. We cannot master cats. Instead they master us.

This book is for cat lovers, cat devotees and people who are willing to admit being mad about cats. There is no criticism whatsoever of cats in it, though such criticism exists. It is, instead, a feast of cat worship, best read with a cat on the lap. Of course, your cat may choose to sit on the page and thus block your view. Some cats enjoy interrupting our reading.

The glory of cats is how effortlessly they upset the traditional hierarchy by treating humans as inferiors. At times I see a kind of compassionate contempt in my cat's eyes. He pities my clumsiness and lack of grace and feline good manners. We humans control and dominate most domestic animals, whether these are pet dogs coming when called, horses saddled for riding, or cattle in a field, fenced by humans to contain them. Cats don't come when called (unless they hear the food bowl); they wriggle out of cat harnesses; and leap over the garden fence whenever they choose.

Though cats live with us, they do not conform to our rules. As Saki wrote; 'The cat is domestic only as far as suits its own ends; it will not be kennelled or harnessed nor suffer any dictation as to its goings out or comings in . . . The social smoothness, the purring innocence, the softness of the velvet paw may be laid aside at a moment's notice, and the sinuous feline may disappear, in deliberate aloofness, to a world of roofs and chimney-stacks, where the human element is distanced and disregarded.'

When I go out into my garden, my cat will suddenly be near me. Where has he been? What was he doing? I do not know. A cat will appear from nowhere and go back into nowhere without its humans ever knowing where it has been or where it is going. It is the cat's nature to be mysterious. Their ways are not our human ways. As Amy Lowell's poem puts it:

In the night, I hear you crying,
But if I try to find you
There are only the shadows of rhododendron leaves

Brushing the ground.
When you come in out of the rain,
All wet and with your tail full of burrs,
You fawn upon me in coils and subtleties . . .

For some of us, the love of our lives begins with a
kitten. 'Kitten is in the animal world what the rosebud
is in the garden; the one the most beautiful of all
young creatures, the other the loveliest of all opening
flowers,' wrote the poet, Robert Southey. He was one
of several authors who mourned that kittens had to
grow up into sober adult cats. The sheer number of
kittens, however, posed a real dilemma for cat lovers in
the days before spaying – a dilemma amusingly
described in verse by the nineteenth-century German
novelist and poet Theodor Storm.

It is in the nature of pet cats to play. Even very
frail old crones of a cat will put a paw out if you trail
some string in front of them. Somewhere in their
psyche is a huge desire to romp, chase, bat at passing
butterflies, skid along wooden floors in pursuit of
shiny balls, or jump up at a fishing rod toy. Cats can

make a toy of anything – an ability we humans might well imitate if we wish to be happy.

So playful verse about cats is part of our childhood heritage. Many nonsense poems about cats find a place in this anthology. Nursery rhymes, like 'Dame Trot and her Wonderful Cat', often have several versions and I have usually just chosen the verses that most entertained me.

Some of the Victorian nursery rhymes, such as 'I love little pussy', were written to encourage kindness to cats; others have a strong moral message about behaviour. Even so 'Mother Tabbyskins', for instance, has a kind of anarchic fantasy despite its apparent moral ending. Perhaps it is one of the nursery rhymes that were bowdlerised or rewritten by Victorians anxious to add the moral. 'Ding, dong bell! Pussy's in the well', a rhyme which may be about 400 years old, originally just ended with the cat being drowned.

Before neutering and spaying, household cats were likely to be female rather than the smellier male. Perhaps this is why nursery cats are often female and sometimes even married to dogs! And I like the way nursery cats often play either a fiddle or bagpipes.

English cathedrals and churches that have carved miserichord seats often show a cat playing a fiddle and these medieval musical cats live on in today's nursery rhymes.

Adults, as well as children, can be childish about cats. Cats bring out the child in their humans. Just the names of cats often show a kind of wild playfulness. Robert Southey's cats included Lord Nelson, Bona Marietta, Bona Fidelia, Madame Catalani, Madame Bianchi, Pulcheria, Ovid, Virgil, Othello, the Zombi, Prester John renamed Pope Joan, Rumpelstilzchen and Hurlyburlypuss. Thomas Hardy had a cat named Kiddleywinkempoops or Trot for short. Mark Twain's cats included Blatherskite, Zoroaster, Sin, Satan, Tammany, Apollinaris, and Sour Mash.

Indeed Mark Twain is the greatest of cat lovers. He always noticed cats on his travels. On a visit to the Sandwich Islands he remarked on the luxurious banks and thickets of flowers, the trees, and the cats – 'Tom-cats, Mary Ann cats, long-tailed cats, bob-tailed cats, blind cats, one-eyed cats, wall-eyed cats, cross-eyed cats, gray cats, black cats, white cats, yellow cats, striped cats, spotted cats, tame cats, wild cats, singed cats, individual cats, groups of cats, platoons of cats, companies of cats, regiments of cats, armies of cats, multitudes of cats, millions of cats, and all of them sleek, fat, lazy and sound asleep.'

It was Twain who realised that every house needed a cat. Inside the house a cat will settle down into the quietest, laziest of beings, even more relaxed than the family dog. There is nothing more soothing than the steady purr of a happy cat lying close by on the bed in the night or on the sofa during the day. As you listen, the curious humming takes away the stress and strain of being human. Walter de la Mare, a sound poet on cats, wrote a charming poem about it.

Puss loves man's winter fire
Now that the sun so soon
Leaves the hours cold it warmed
In burning June.

She purrs full length before
The heaped-up hissing blaze,
Drowsy in slumber down
Her head she lays.

While he with whom she dwells
Sits snug in his inglenook,
Stretches his legs to the flame
And reads his book.

I enjoy the steady purr of a cat but even more my heart is taken by the wildness, which lies beneath that apparent serenity. Cats are supreme predators, dedicated to hunting and designed to do the hunting sequence of eye, stalk, pounce and bite. The most domestic of kitties has a ruthless tiger's heart. This may not be obvious to the owners of those cats who spend the whole of their lives indoors. Were they, however, to let a mouse into the flat (and I hope nobody would deliberately do such a cruel act) they will see their fluffy loving cat turn immediately into a murderer. Killing is what cats do best and, although I mourn for the little animals and birds killed by my cat, I marvel at his predatory nature. A cat is truly 'a diminutive lion'.

When we look at the cat–human relationship, we see something very odd indeed – not in the cat, but in ourselves. Some of us (myself very definitely included) move from the respectable love of a domestic animal to a kind of obsessed adoration. Do we go too far? Well, some of us (again myself included) probably do. As a cat behaviour counsellor, I am amazed at what cat owners will put up with for years – cats that bite their humans, cats that claw the wallpaper into shreds and cats that spray urine round the house.

In a 1938 copy of 'Notes and Queries', a correspondent wrote: 'I read somewhere – in Lord Broughton's Memoirs, I think – of an old lady who prepared a Christmas tree for her cats. It was hung with herrings and they walked round it solemnly before being presented with the special delights it supplied. They must have been well trained not to spring up and detach the fish.'

After several years of searching I think I have now tracked down the cat owner who provided the fishy Christmas tree – not an old lady but an eccentric Victorian clergyman, Sabine Baring Gould. His account of a cat Christmas tree can be found in chapter six.

He is not alone in his feline enthusiasm. Garden designer Gertrude Jekyll was so mad about cats that she gave hers a special tea party. Cardinal Richelieu left pensions to his fourteen cats at the time of his death, and during his life servants were assigned to care for them. The novelist and poet, Thomas Hardy, whose cat poems are in this anthology, used to entertain several cats to tea. A visitor once asked him if this army of cats were all his own, and he explained that while his own cats were there, the others included cats who visited regularly at tea time, and others who had just turned up.

The poet, John Keats, like Mark Twain, had an eye for cats. He noticed the cats at his various lodgings and wrote a poem about one of them – 'To Mrs Reynolds's Cat' – which is in chapter six. He once fought a butcher's boy (and the fight went on for nearly an hour) because he saw him tormenting a kitten. Another devotee was the nonsense poet and illustrator Edward Lear, who adored his cat, Foss. When he moved house he ordered the builder of his new house to make it exactly like his old one, so that Foss would feel at home. Foss lived to the immense age of thirty-one and perhaps it was no coincidence that Edward Lear himself died only a few months later.

Many much-loved cats seem to develop into a larger-than-life personality. The devotion of their owners helps them blossom into their true selves. Among cats, as among people, there are individuals whose towering personalities stand out from the crowd. Trim, the sea cat belonging to Captain Matthews Flinders, is one and, if this were a bigger book, I would have used every word of Captain's Flinders' account of this remarkable cat. As it is, a shorter account of Trim can be found in chapter seven.

In the Royal Navy cats have always had distinguished careers, keeping the huge warships free of rats. Even in World War Two, cats sailed with the fleet on destroyers and battleships, as Commander William Donald, now alas dead, recalled for me in words he wrote for me in 1993.

Some cats joined the Army, like Crimea Tom whose stuffed body is to be seen in the National Army Museum in London. Others have taken up duties as mousing operatives in stables and, in the course of their duties, made friends with horses like The Arabian, the famous racehorse who was founder of the thoroughbred breed. There are cats too who have gone into the theatre and made their mark backstage – like Gertie, official stage cat of the Phoenix Theatre in the 1990s.

No cat is quite like another cat, which is perhaps why those grieving the loss of a cat can feel so hurt when told, 'Get another one.' As I worked on this book, I lost my beautiful young black cat, George. So the elegies on the deaths of cats spoke to my heart more directly than ever before. Even so, some of the extracts and poems about death have an element of humour. George, the most playful cat I have ever known, would have appreciated that. He enjoyed making me laugh. Margaret Atwood's story, 'Our Cat Goes to Heaven' is one of the funniest I have read. I only hope that George has arrived at that kind of feline heaven.

All long love affairs end in sorrow and loss. We pay for love in tears and it is worth the price. I have a hope, a very slight and uncertain hope, that I might one day find George waiting for me in heaven. If he, and Moppet and Dear Little Mog and Fat Ada are not there, I don't want to be there myself. For me heaven has to have cats.

The Nature of Cats

The smallest feline is a masterpiece.

🐾 *Leonardo da Vinci* (1452–1519),
   artist and scientist

Cats have dark and impenetrable little souls,
souls that are tender, proud and fey. They reveal
themselves only to a privileged few, shunning the
slightest impropriety and the mildest deception.
Their intelligence is at least equal to that of dogs,
though they never exhibit any of the latter's
obsequious submission nor their ridiculous self-
importance and revolting vulgarity. Cats are
elegant and patrician beasts; dogs, on the contrary,
regardless of their social position, retain all the

shoddiness of social upstarts and remain irremediably common.

🐾 *Pierre Loti* *(Louis Marie Julien Viaud)*
(1850–1923), writer

Cat,
Cat,
What are you?
Son, through a thousand generations, of the black
   leopards
Padding among the springs of young bamboo;
Descendant of many removals from the white
   panthers
Who crouch by night under the loquat-trees?
You crouch under the orange begonias,
And your eyes are green
With the violence of murder,
Or half-closed and stealthy
Like your sheathed claws.
Slowly, slowly,
You rise and stretch

In a glossiness of beautiful curves,
Of muscles fluctuating under black, glazed hair . . .

In the night, I hear you crying,
But if I try to find you
There are only the shadows of rhododendron leaves
Brushing the ground.
When you come in out of the rain,
All wet and with your tail full of burrs,
You fawn upon me in coils and subtleties;
But once you are dry
You leave me with a gesture of inconceivable
    impudence,
Conveyed by the vanishing quirk of your tail
As you slide through the open door.

You walk as a king scorning his subjects;
You flirt with me as a concubine in robes of silk.
Cat,
I am afraid of your poisonous beauty,
I have seen you torturing a mouse.
Yet when you lie purring in my lap
I forget everything but how soft you are,

And it is only when I feel your claws open upon my
    hand
That I remember –

Remember a puma lying out on a branch above my
    head
Years ago.

Shall I choke you, Cat,
Or kiss you?
Really I do not know.

🐾 *Amy Lowell* (1874–1925), 'To Winky'

In the political history of nations it is no uncommon
experience to find States and peoples which but a
short time since were in bitter conflict and animosity
with each other, settled down comfortably on terms
of mutual goodwill and even alliance. The natural
history of the social developments of species affords a
similar instance in the coming-together of two once
warring elements, now represented by civilized man

and the domestic cat. The fiercely waged struggle
which went on between humans and felines in those
far-off days when sabre-toothed tiger and cave lion
contended with primeval man, has long ago been
decided in favour of the most fitly equipped combat-
ant – the Thing with a Thumb – and the descendants
of the dispossessed family are relegated today, for the
most part, to the waste lands of jungle and veld,
where an existence of self-effacement is the only
alternative to extermination. But the *felis catus*, or
whatever species was the ancestor of the modern
domestic cat (a vexed question at present), by a
master-stroke of adaptation avoided the ruin of its
race, and 'captured' a place in the very keystone of the
conqueror's organization. For not as a bond-servant
or dependent has this proudest of mammals entered
the human fraternity; not as a slave like the beasts of
burden, or a humble camp-follower like the dog. The
cat is domestic only as far as suits its own ends; it
will not be kennelled or harnessed nor suffer any
dictation as to its goings out or comings in. Long
contact with the human race has developed in it the
art of diplomacy, and no Roman Cardinal of mediæval

days knew better how to ingratiate himself with his surroundings than a cat with a saucer of cream on its mental horizon. But the social smoothness, the purring innocence, the softness of the velvet paw may be laid aside at a moment's notice, and the sinuous feline may disappear, in deliberate aloofness, to a world of roofs and chimney-stacks, where the human element is distanced and disregarded. Or the innate savage spirit that helped its survival in the bygone days of tooth and claw may be summoned forth from beneath the sleek exterior, and the torture-instinct (common alone to human and feline) may find free play in the death-throes of some luckless bird or rodent. It is, indeed, no small triumph to have combined the untrammelled liberty of primeval savagery with the luxury which only a highly developed civilization can command; to be lapped in the soft stuffs that commerce has gathered from the far ends of the world, to bask in the warmth that labour and industry have dragged from the bowels of the earth; to banquet on the dainties that wealth has bespoken for its table, and withal to be a free son of nature, a mighty hunter, a spiller of life-blood. This is the victory of the cat. But besides the credit of success the cat has other qualities which compel recognition. The animal which the Egyptians worshipped as divine, which the Romans venerated as a symbol of liberty, which Europeans in the ignorant Middle Ages anathematized as an agent of demonology, has displayed to all ages two closely blended characteristics – courage and self-respect. No matter how unfavourable the circumstances, both qualities are always to the fore. Confront a child, a puppy, and a kitten with a sudden danger; the child will turn instinctively for assistance, the puppy will grovel in abject submission to the impending visitation, the kitten will brace its tiny body for a frantic resistance.

👣 'Saki' *(Hector Hugh Munro) (1870–1916)*, writer

To respect the cat is the beginning of the aesthetic sense.

👣 Erasmus Darwin *(1731–1802)*, poet and scientist

For I will consider my Cat Jeoffry.

For he is the servant of the Living God, duly and daily serving him.

For at the first glance of the glory of God in the East he worships in his way.

For is this done by wreathing his body seven times round with elegant quickness.

For then he leaps up to catch the musk, which is the blessing of God upon his prayer.

For he rolls upon prank to work it in.

For having done duty and received blessing he begins to consider himself.

For this he performs in ten degrees.

For first he looks upon his fore paws to see if they are clean.

For secondly he kicks up behind to clear away there.

For thirdly he works it upon stretch with the fore paws extended.

For fourthly he sharpens his paws by wood.

For fifthly he washes himself.

For sixthly he rolls upon wash.

For seventhly he fleas himself, that he may not be interrupted upon the beat.

For eighthly he rubs himself against a post.

For ninthly he looks up for his instructions.

For tenthly he goes in quest of food.

For having considered God and himself he will consider his neighbour.

For if he meets another cat he will kiss her in kindness.

For when he takes his prey he plays with it to give it a chance.

For one mouse in seven escapes by his dallying.

For when his day's work is done his business more properly begins.

For he keeps the Lord's watch in the night against the adversary.

For he counteracts the powers of darkness by his electrical skin and glaring eyes.

For he counteracts the Devil, who is death, by brisking about the life.

For in his morning orisons he loves the sun and the sun loves him.

For he is of the tribe of Tiger.

For the Cherub Cat is a term of the Angel Tiger.

For he has the subtlety and hissing of a serpent, which in goodness he suppresses.

For he will not do destruction, if he is well fed,
neither will he spit without provocation.
For he purrs in thankfulness, when God tells him
he's a good cat.
And he is an instrument for the children to learn
benevolence upon.
For every house in incomplete without him and a
blessing is lacking in the spirit.
For the Lord commanded Moses concerning the cats
at the departure of the Children of Israel from
Egypt.
For every family had one cat at least in the bag.
For the English cats are the best in Europe.

🐾 *Christopher Smart (1722–1771)*, 'Jubilate Deo'

Who can tell what just criticism Murr the cat may be
passing on us beings of wider speculation?

🐾 *George Eliot (1819–1888)*, novelist

Little cat,
little cat,
walking so alone,
tell me whose
cat are you?
– I'm damned well my own.

🐾 *Piet Hein (1905–1996)*, 'Littlecat'

The Turks greatly admire cats; to them, their alluring
figure appears preferable to the docility, instinct, and
fidelity of the dog. Mahomet was very partial to cats.
It is related, that being called up on some urgent
business, he preferred cutting off the sleeve of his
robe, to waking the cat, that lay upon it asleep.
Nothing more was necessary to bring these animals
into high request. A cat may even enter a mosque; it
is caressed there, as the favourite animal of the
prophet.

🐾 *Rev. William Daniel*, 'Rural Sports', 1813

The man who carries a cat by the tail learns a lesson that can be learned no other way.

🐾 *Mark Twain* *(1835–1910)*, novelist and humourist

When a cat caresses you, it never looks at you. Its heart seems to be in its back and paws, not its eyes. It will rub itself against you, or pat you with velvet tufts, instead of talons, but you may talk to it for an hour altogether, yet not rightly catch its eye.

🐾 *John Ruskin* *(1819–1900)*, writer and art critic

The cat laps the moon-beams in the bowl of water,
Thinking them to be milk,

A ray is caught in a bowl,
And the cat licks it, thinking that it's milk.

Look at the cloud-cat, lapping there on high
With lightening tongue the moon milk from the sky.

🐾 *Yoesvara, tr. John Brough*, 'Poems
from the Sanskrit', 1968

The fur of the cat, being generally clean and dry,
readily yields electric sparks when rubbed; and, if a
clean and perfectly dry domestic cat be placed, in
frosty weather, on a stool with glass feet, or be insu-
lated by any other means, and rubbed for a little time
in contact with the wire of a coated phial, the phial
will become charged.

🐾 *Rev. William Bingley*, 'Animal Biography',
1805

You've read of several kinds of Cat,
And my opinion now is that
You should need no interpreter
To understand their character.

You now have learned enough to see
That Cats are much like you and me
And other people whom we find
Possessed of various types of mind.
For some are sane and some are mad
And some are good and some are bad
And some are better, some are worse—
But all may be described in verse.
You've seen them both at work and games,
And learnt about their proper names,
Their habits and their habitat:
But

How would you ad-dress a Cat?
So first, your memory I'll jog,
And say: A CAT IS NOT A DOG.

Now Dogs pretend they like to fight;
They often bark, more seldom bite;
But yet a Dog is, on the whole,
What you would call a simple soul.
Of course I'm not including Pekes,
And such fantastic canine freaks.
The usual Dog about the Town
Is much inclined to play the clown,

And far from showing too much pride
Is frequently undignified.
He's very easily taken in –
Just chuck him underneath the chin
Or slap his back or shake his paw,
And he will gambol and guffaw.
He's such an easy-going lout,
He'll answer any hail or shout.

Again I must remind you that
A Dog's a Dog – A CAT'S A CAT.

With Cats, some say, one rule is true:
Don't speak till you are spoken to.
Myself, I do not hold with that –
I say, you should ad-dress a Cat.
But always keep in mind that he
Resents familiarity.
I bow, and taking off my hat,
Ad-dress him in this form: O CAT!
But if he is the Cat next door,
Whom I have often met before
(He comes to see me in my flat)
I greet him with an OOPSA CAT!

I think I've heard them call him James –
But we've not got so far as names.
Before a Cat will condescend
To treat you as a trusted friend,
Some little token of esteem
Is needed, like a dish of cream;
And you might now and then supply
Some caviare, or Strassburg Pie,
Some potted grouse, or salmon paste—
He's sure to have his personal taste.
(I know a Cat, who makes a habit
Of eating nothing else but rabbit,
And when he's finished, licks his paws
So's not to waste the onion sauce.)
A Cat's entitled to expect
These evidences of respect.
And so in time you reach your aim,
And finally call him by his NAME.

So this is this, and that is that:
And there's how you AD-DRESS A CAT.

🐾 *T.S. Eliot* *(1888–1965),* 'The Ad-dressing of
Cats'

I've met many thinkers and many cats, but the wisdom of cats is infinitely superior.

🐾 *Hippolyte Taine* (1828–1893), historian and critic

A dog will often steal a bone,
But conscience lets him not alone,
And by his tail his guilt is known.

But cats consider theft a game
And, howsoever you may blame,
Refuse the slightest sign of shame.

When food mysteriously goes,
The chances are that Pussy knows
More than she leads you to suppose.

And hence there is no need for you,
If Puss declines a meal or two,
To feel her pulse or make ado.

🐾 *Anonymous*

The Cat is most like to the leopard, and hath a great mouth, and saw-teeth and sharp, and a long tongue, and pliant, thin and subtle. He lappeth therewith when he drinketh, as other beasts do that have the nether lip shorter than the over; for, because of unevenness of lips such beasts suck not in drinking, but lap and lick, as Aristotle saith, and Plinius also. And he is a full lecherous beast in youth, swift, pliant and merry, and leapeth, and riseth on all things that are tofore him; and is led by a straw, and playeth therewith; and is a right heavy beast in age, and fully sleepy, and lyeth slyly in waite for mice; and is ware where they bene more by smell than by sight, and hunteth, and riseth on them in privy places; and when he taketh a mouse he playeth therewith, and eateth him after the play . . .

🐾 **Bartholomeus Anglicus, tr.**
Thomas Berthlet, 'De Proprietatibus Rerum', 1498

I'll study thee, Puss! . . .

   Come, look at me; . . .

Lift up thine emerald eyes! Aye purr away!

For I am praising thee, I tell thee, Puss

And cats as well as kings like flattery . . .

   What a power there is

In beauty! Within these forbidden walls

Thou hast thy range at will, and when perchance

The Fellows see thee, Puss, they overlook

Inhibitory laws or haply think

The statute was not made for cats like thee;

For thou art beautiful as ever cat

That wantoned in the joy of kittenhood.

Aye, stretch thy claws, thou democratic beast, . . .

I like thine independence. Treat thee well,

Thou are as playful as young innocence;

But if we act the governor, and break

The social compact, Nature gave those claws

And taught thee how to use them. Man, methinks,

Master and slave alike, might learn from thee

A salutary lesson: but the one

Abuses wickedly his power unjust,

The other crouches, spaniel-like, and licks

The hand that strikes him. Wiser animal,
I look at thee, familiarized, yet free . . .

🐾 **Robert Southey**, 'Installation at Oxford', 1793

Of all animals, he alone attains the Contemplative
Life.

🐾 **Andrew Lang** *(1844–1912)*, essayist and author

I am the cat of cats, I am
The everlasting cat!
Cunning and old, and sleek as jam,
The everlasting cat!
I hunt the vermin in the night –
The everlasting cat!
For I see best without the light –
The everlasting cat.

🐾 **William Brighty Rands** *(1823–1882)*, 'The
Cat of Cats'

I beg leave to communicate to the Society an easy method of preserving fruit trees and gardens from the depredation of birds, as adopted by my friend, Robert Brooke, Esq. . . . He has four of five cats, each with a collar, a light chain and swivel, about a yard long with a large iron ring at the end; as soon as gooseberries, currants and raspberries begin to ripen, a small stake is driven into the ground, or bed, near the trees to be protected, leaving about a yard and a half of the stake above ground; the ring is slipped over the head of the stake, and the cat thus tethered in the sight of trees, no birds will approach them. Cherry trees and wall fruit trees are protected in the same manner as they successively ripen; each cat, by way of a shed, has one of the largest sized flower pots laid on its side, within reach of its chain, with a little hay or straw in bad weather, and her food and water placed near her.

🐾 *Anonymous,* 'Transactions of the Horticultural Society', 1832

We cats, when assembled at midnight together
For innocent purring, purring
On moon-shiney weather,
If dogs be in kennel all fast in their straw,
We march, and we meow without scratch or a claw.
But if they surprise us and put us to flight,
We fret, fret and we spit, fret, spit, spit,
Give a squall, squall, and good night.

🐾 *Richard Brown* (d. 1710), 'A Cat Catch'

As for cats, they nearly equal human beings for
vanity. I have known a cat get up and walk out of the
room, on a remark derogatory to her species being
made by a visitor, while a neatly turned compliment
will set them purring for an hour.

I do like cats. They are so unconsciously amusing.
There is such a comic dignity about them, such a
'How dare you!' 'Go away, don't touch me' sort of air
. . . When you want to win the approbation of a cat
you must mind what you are about, and work your way
carefully. If you don't know the cat, you had best begin

by saying, 'Poor pussy'. After which add, 'Did'ums', in a tone of soothing sympathy. You don't know what you mean, any more than the cat does, but the sentiment seems to imply a proper spirit on your part, and generally touches her feelings to such an extent that, if you are of good manners and passable appearance, she will stick her back up and rub her nose against you. Matters having reached this stage, you may venture to chuck her under the chin, and tickle the side of her head, and the intelligent creature will then stick her claws into your legs; and all is friendship and affection . . .

Cats have the credit of being more worldly wise than dogs – of looking more after their own interest, and being less blindly devoted to those of their friends. And we men and women are naturally shocked at such self-ishness. Cats certainly do love a family that has a carpet in the kitchen more than a family that has not; and if there are many children about, they prefer to spend their leisure time next door. But, taken altogether, cats are libelled. Make a friend of one, and she will stick to you through thick and thin.

🐾 *Jerome K Jerome* (1859–1927), author and humourist

Incorrigible, uncommitted,
They leavened the long flat hours of my childhood,
Subtle, the opposite of dogs,
And, unlike dogs, capable
Of flirting, falling, and yawning anywhere,
Like women who want no contract
But going their own way
Make the way of their lovers lighter.

🐾 *Louis Macneice* (1907–1964), 'Nature Notes:
   Cats'

The cat is particularly averse to water, cold, and bad
smells. It is fond of certain perfumes, but is more
particularly attracted by the smell of valerian, marum,
and cat-mint: it rubs itself against them; and, if not
prevented from coming at them in a garden where
they are planted, would infallibly destroy them.

🐾 *Thomas Bewick*, 'A General History of
   Quadrupeds', 1807

The dog is really useful, for he helps to guard the
    house,
And he'll carry your umbrella or your glove;
But a cat does simply nothing save to catch the
    luckless mouse,
Which no one could account an act of love.

🐾 *Anonymous*

There is the fable, Chinese I think, literary I am sure:
of a period on earth when the dominant creatures
were cats: who after ages of trying to cope with the
anguishes of mortality – famine, plague, war,
injustice, folly, greed – in a word, civilized government – convened a congress of the wisest cat
philosophers to see if anything could be done: who
after long deliberation agreed that the dilemma, the
problems themselves were insoluble and the only
practical solution was to give it up, relinquish,
abdicate, by selecting from among the lesser
creatures a species, race optimistic enough to believe
that the mortal predicament could be solved and

ignorant enough never to learn better. Which is why the cat lives with you, is completely dependent on you for food and shelter but lifts no paw for you and loves you not; in a word, why your cat looks at you the way it does.

🐾 **William Faulkner**, 'The Reivers', 1962

To err is human
To purr feline.

🐾 **Robert Byrne** *(b. 1928)*, author

There are many household animals; and there would be many more, were it not for what happens to the cats. When the females have kittened, they will not consort with the males; and these seek them but cannot get their will of them; so their device is to steal and carry off and kill the kittens (but they do not eat what they have killed). The mothers, deprived of their young and desiring to have more, will then consort with the males; for they are creatures that love offspring. And when a fire breaks out very strange things happen to the cats. The Egyptians stand round in a broken line, thinking more of the cats than of quenching the burning; but the cats slip through or leap over the men and spring into the fire. When this happens, there is great mourning in Egypt. Dwellers in a house where a cat has died a natural death shave their eyebrows and no more; where a dog has so died, the head and the whole body are shaven.

Dead cats are taken away into sacred buildings, where they are embalmed and buried, in the town of Bubastis . . .

🐾 *Herodotus* *(c.484–c.425 BC)*, Greek historian

Under a tree I read a Latin Book,
And there in seeming slumber, lies my cat;
Each of us thinking, with our harmless look.
Of this and that.

Such singing – prettier than any words –
O singers you are sweet and well-to-do!
My cat, who has the finest taste in birds,
Thinks so too.

🐾 *Dugald S MacColl* *(1859–1948)*, 'Connoisseurs'

A cat, when feeling affectionate . . . stands upright,
with slightly arched back, tail perpendicularly raised,
and ears erected; and she rubs her cheeks and flanks
against her master or mistress. The desire to rub
something is so strong in cats under this state of
mind, that they may often be seen rubbing themselves
against the legs of chairs or tables, or against door-
posts. This manner of expressing affection probably
originated through association . . . from the mother
nursing and fondling her young; and perhaps from
the young themselves loving each other and playing
together. Another and very different gesture,
expressive of pleasure, has already been described,
namely, the curious manner in which young and even
old cats, when pleased, alternately protrude their

fore-feet, with separated toes, as if pushing against and sucking their mother's teats. This habit is so far analogous to that of rubbing against something, that both apparently are derived from actions performed during the nursing period. Why cats should show affection by rubbing so much more than do dogs, though the latter delight in contact with their masters, and why cats only occasionally lick the hands of their friends, whilst dogs always do so, I cannot say.

🐾 **Charles Darwin**, 'The Expressions of the Emotions in Man and Animals', 1872

Though cat (a good mouser) is jewel in house
Yet every in dairy have trap for a mouse.

🐾 **Thomas Tusser**, 'Five Hundred Points of Good Husbandry', 1557

'We're all mad here, I'm mad. You're mad,' said the Cat. 'How do you know I'm mad?' said Alice.

'You must be,' said the Cat, 'or you wouldn't have come here.'

Alice didn't think that proved it at all: however, she went on: 'And how do you know that you're mad?'

'To begin with,' said the Cat, 'a dog's not mad. You grant that?'

'I suppose so,' said Alice.

'Well, then,' the Cat went on, 'you see a dog growls when it's angry, and wags its tail when it's pleased. Now I growl when I'm pleased, and wag my tail when I'm angry. Therefore, I am mad.'

'I call it purring, not growling,' said Alice.

'Call it what you like,' said the Cat.

🐾 *Lewis Carroll* (*Charles Lutwidge Dodgson*), 'Alice in Wonderland', 1865

The Cheshire Cat?
Clever.
– But every cat knows the trick of disappearance.

🐾 *Pam Brown*, living author

46

It seemed a scholar and his cat
Together joined in social chat . . .
With visage placid and sedate,
Puss thus addressed her learned mate:
'We're told that none in nature's plan
Disputes pre-eminence with man.
But this is still a dubious case
To me, and all our purring race.
We grant indeed to partial eyes
Men may appear supremely wise.
But our sagacious rabbis hold,
That all which glitters is not gold.
Pray, if your haughty claims be true,
Why are our manners aped by you?
Whene'er you think, all cats agree,
You shut your optics just as we.
Pray, why like cats so rapt in thought
If you by cats were never taught?
But know our tabby schools maintain
Worth is not centered in the brain . . . '

🐾 *Charles Cotton* (1630–1687), poet

I prefer certainly to have neither cat nor dog, but were I forced to live with one of these two individuals, I would choose the cat. It has for me the manners essential to social relations. At first, in its early youth, it possesses all the graces, all the suppleness, all the unexpectedness by which the most exacting, artistic fancy can be amused! It is adroit, it always knows where it is. Prudent unto caution, it goes everywhere, it examines without soiling, breaking nothing: it is in itself a warmth and a caress; it has not a snout, but a mouth – and what a mouth! It steals the mutton as does the dog, but, unlike the later, makes no delight of carrion; it is discreet and of fastidious cleanliness, which might be well imitated by some of its detractors. It washes its face, and in so doing foretells the weather into the bargain. One can entertain the idea of putting a ribbon around its neck, never a collar; it cannot be enslaved. It permits no modifications in its race; it lends itself to no combinations that industry could attempt . . . in short, the cat is a dignified, proud, disdainful animal that hides its love affairs in the shadows, almost within the clouds, upon the roofs, in the vicinity of the night-working students. It defies advances, tolerates no insults, it abandons the house in which it is not treated according to its merits; in short, the cat is truly an aristocrat in type and origin . . .

🐾 *Alexandre Dumas* *(1802–1870)*, novelist

We cannot, of course, without becoming cats, perfectly understand the cat mind.

🐾 *St George Mivart*, 'The Cat', 1881

It is a beast of prey, even the tame one, more especially the wild, it being in the opinion of many nothing but a diminutive lion . . . It has a broad face almost like a lion, short ears, large whiskers, shining eyes, short smooth hair, long tail, rough tongue, and armed on its feet with claws, being a crafty, subtle, watchful Creature, very loving and familiar with mankind, the mortal enemy to the rat, mouse, and all sorts of birds,

which it seizes on as its prey. As to its eyes, authors
say that they shine in the night; and see better at the
full, and more dimly at the change of the moon.

🐾 **William Salmon**, 'The English physician', 1693

Tearaway kitten or staid mother of fifty,
Persian, Chinchilla, Siamese
Or backstreet brawler – you all have tiger in your
    blood
And eyes opaque as the sacred mysteries.

The hunter's instinct sends you pouncing, dallying,
Formal and wild as a temple dance.
You take from man what is your due – the fireside
    saucer,
And give him his – a purr of tolerance.

Like poets you wrap your solitude around you
And catch your meaning unawares:
With consequential trot or frantic tarantella
You follow up your top-secret affairs.

Simpkin, our pretty cat, assumes my lap
As a princess her rightful throne,
Pads round and drops asleep there. Each is a familiar
Warmth to the other, each no less alone.

🐾 **C. Day-Lewis** *(1904–1972)*, 'Cat'

Chapter Five

Kittens

A house is never perfectly furnished for enjoyment,
unless there is a child in it rising three years old, and
a kitten rising six weeks . . .

   Kitten is in the animal world what the rosebud is
in the garden; the one the most beautiful of all young
creatures, the other the loveliest of all opening flowers.
The rose loses only something in delicacy by its
development, – enough to make it a serious emblem
to the pensive mind; but if a cat could remember
kittenhood, as we remember our youth, it were
enough to break a cat's heart, even if it had nine
times nine heart strings.

Robert Southey *(1774–1843)*, poet and author

55

God at first the sun created
Then each nightly constellation;
From the sweat of his own forehead
Oxen were his next creation.

Wild beasts he created later,
Lions with their paws so furious;
In the image of the lion.
Made he kittens small and curious.

🐾 *Heinrich Heine* (1797–1856), poet

The weeping willow changed its shape when a cruel human threw a litter of kittens into the river. The mother cat mewed so piteously that the willow bent down to the water, so that the kittens could cling to its branches and be saved.

🐾 *Polish folk tale.*

Nothing's more playful than a young cat, nor more grave than an old one.

🐾 *Rev. Thomas Fuller* (1608–1661), historian

I have a kitten, my dear, the drollest of all creatures that ever wore a cat's skin. Her gambols are not to be described, and would be incredible, if they could. She tumbles head over heels several times together, she lays her cheek to the ground and presents her rump at you with an air of most supreme disdain, from this posture she rises to dance on her hind feet, an exercise she performs with all the grace imaginable, and she closes those various exhibitions with a loud smack of her lips, which for want of greater propriety of expression we call spitting. But though all cats spit, no cat ever produced such a sound as she does. For point of size she is likely to be a kitten always, being extremely small of her age, but time I suppose, that spoils everything, will make her also a cat. You will see her I hope before that melancholy period shall arrive, for no wisdom that she may gain by experience, and reflect hereafter, will compensate the loss of her present hilarity. She is dressed in a tortoiseshell suit, and I know that you will like her.

🐾 *William Cowper*, Letter to Lady Hesketh, 1787

The trouble with a kitten is
THAT
Eventually it becomes a
CAT.

🐾 *Ogden Nash (1902–1971)*, 'The Kitten'

Kittenhood, the baby time especially of country cats, is with most the brightest, sprightliest, and prettiest period of their existence and perhaps the most happy. True, when first born and in the earliest era of their lives, they are blind, helpless little things, dull, weak, and staggering, scarcely able to stand, if at all, almost rolling over at every attempt, making querulous, fretful noises, if wakeful or cold, or for the time motherless.

But 'tis not for long; awhile, and she, the fondest of mothers, is with them. They are nestled about her, or amid her soft, warm fluffy fur, cossetted with parental tenderness, caressed, nurtured, and, with low sweet tones and fondlings, they are soothed again and again to sleep. – They sleep. – Noiseless, and with many a longing, lingering look, the careful, watchful, loving creature slowly and reluctantly steals away; soon to return, when she and her little ones are lost 'in the land of dreams.' And so from day to day, until bright, meek-eyed, innocent, inquiring little faces, with eager eyes, peep above the basket that is yet their home. One bolder than the others springs out, when, scared at its own audacity, as quickly, and oft clumsily, scrambles back, then out – in – and out, in happy, varied, wild, frolicsome, gambolsome play, they clutch, twist, turn, and wrestle in artless mimicry of desperate quarrelling; – the struggle over, in liveliest antics they chase and rechase in turn, or in fantastic mood play; 'tis but play, and such wondrous play – bright, joyous, and light; and so life glides on with them as kittens – frisky, skittish, playful kittens.

🐾 *Harrison Weir*, 'Our Cats', 1889

The little kitten's face
Like the sudden dawn
Swallows all of midnight
With a big pink yawn.

🐾 *Anonymous*

A kitten is the delight of the household. Where there is one of these little creatures, a play is being performed all day long by the incomparable actor. Searchers for perpetual motion need do no more than observe a kitten. Its stage is always ready . . . It needs but a few properties; a scrap of paper, a pen, a piece of string, a pincushion, are quite enough for it to accomplish prodigies of posturing . . .

Even when a kitten is quiet, nothing can be more amusing. The little crouching creature with its shut eyes has such a knowing touch-me-not air. Its head hanging as though overwhelmed with sleep, its stretched-out paws, its dainty little nose, all seem to say 'Don't wake me, I am so happy.' A sleeping kitten is the image of perfect beatitude . . .

There are no more intrepid explorers than kittens. They make voyages of discovery into cellars and garrets, they climb on the roofs of neighbouring houses, put their little noses out of half-closed street doors, and return with a store of observation laid up for future use.

Sometimes, however, this ardent curiosity leads them into dangerous places, and brings them into difficulties which they have cause to regret.

It is worthwhile to watch a kitten climbing a tree. Up it goes, from branch to branch, higher and higher, as though to enjoy the spectacle of a grand panorama. Where is it going to? It knows not. It climbs eagerly, heedless of the diminishing size of the branches, and it is only when it lays its paws upon the frail upper twigs that it begins to understand the danger of its going always straight ahead. Then it is seized with terror, and being unable to continue its course, mews in a heart-rending manner. If the tree upon which it is perched in consternation be too lofty to admit of a ladder being brought to aid in the salvage of the poor little animal, the kitten with infinite precautions, and a heart beating almost out of its body, will let itself slide along the branches sticking its nervously convulsed claws in them . . .

🐾 **Champfleury** (Jules Fleury-Husson), 'The Cat Past and Present', 1885

Can he name a kitten? By this test I am condemned, for I cannot.

🐾 **Samuel Butler** *(1835–1902), novelist*

A kitten is so flexible that she is almost double; the hind parts are equivalent to another kitten with which the forepart plays. She does not discover that her tail belongs to her until you tread on it.

🐾 **Henry David Thoreau** *(1817–1862),*
philosopher

That way look, my Infant, lo!
What a pretty baby-show!

See the kitten on the wall,
Sporting with the leaves that fall,
Withered leaves – one – two – and three –
From the lofty elder tree! . . .
– But the kitten, how she starts,
Crouches, stretches, paws and darts!
First at one, and then its fellow,
Just as light, and just as yellow;
There are many now – now one –
Now they stop and there are none:
What intenseness of desire
In her upward eye of fire!
With a tiger-leap half-way,
Now she meets the coming prey,
Lets it go as fast, and then
Has it in her power again.
Now she works with three or four,
Like an Indian conjurer:
Quick as he in feats of art,
Far beyond in joy of heart.
Were her antics played in the eye
Of a thousand standers-by,
Clapping hands with shout and stare,
What would little Tabby care

For the plaudits of the crowd?
Over happy to be proud,
Over wealthy in the treasure
Of her own exceeding pleasure! . . .

Such a light of gladness breaks,
Pretty kitten! from thy freaks, –
Spreads with such a living grace
O'er my little Dora's face;
Yes, the sight so stirs and charms
Thee, Baby, laughing in my arms,
That almost I could repine
That your transports are not mine . . .
Now and then I may possess
Hours of perfect gladsomeness,
– Pleased by any random toy;
By a kitten's busy joy,
Or an infant's laughing eye
Sharing in the ecstasy;
I would fare like that or this,
Find my wisdom in my bliss;
Keep the sprightly soul awake,
And have faculties to take,

Even from things by sorrow wrought,
Matter for a jocund thought,
Spite of care, and spite of grief,
To gambol with Life's falling leaf.

🐾 **William Wordsworth**, 'The Kitten and
Falling Leaves', 1807

Trains seem to have a special fascination for cats,
and they are often to be seen about stations. For a
long while one was regularly to be seen travelling
on the Metropolitan line, between St. James's Park
and Charing Cross, and a whole family of half-wild
kittens are at this moment making a playground of
the lines and platforms at Paddington. One will curl
up quite comfortably on the line right under the
wheel of a carriage that is just going to start, and
on being disturbed bolts away and hides itself in
some recess underneath the platform. Occasionally
you see one with part of its tail cut off, but as a
rule they take wonderfully good care of themselves.
The porters are very kind to them, and they

somehow contrive to get along, for they all look fat and well-looking, and quite happy in their strange quarters.

🐾 *Andrew Lang*, 'The Animal Story Book', 1896

I'd rather be a kitten and cry, Mew! than write the best poetry in the world.

🐾 *Sir Walter Scott*, Letter to Allan Cunningham, 1822

If I can find a photograph of my 'Tammany' and her kittens, I will enclose it in this. One of them likes to be crammed into a corner pocket of the billiard table – which he fits as snugly as does a finger in a glove, and then he watches the game (and obstructs it) by the hour, and spoils many a shot by putting out his paw and changing the direction of a passing ball. Whenever a ball is in his arms, or so close to him that it cannot be layed upon without the risk of hurting

him, the player is privileged to remove it to any of
the three spots that chances to be open.

🐾 *Mark Twain (Samuel Langhorne Clemens)*,
    Letter to Mrs Patterson, 1908

Kitten, Kitten, two months old,
Woolly snow-ball, lying snug,
Curled up in the warmest fold
Of the warm hearth-rug,
Turn your drowsy head this way.
What is life? Oh, Kitten, say!

'Life!' said the kitten, winking her eyes,
And twitching her tail, in a droll surprise –
'Life? – Oh, it's racing over the floor,
Out at the window and in at the door;
Now on the chair back, now on the table,
'Mid balls of cotton and skeins of silk,
And crumbs of sugar and jugs of milk.'

🐾 *Thomas Westwood (1814–1858)*, poet

Ah me! Life sadly changes us all. The world seems a vast horrible grinding machine, into which what is fresh and bright and pure is pushed at one end, to come out old and crabbed and wrinkled at the other.

Look even at Pussy Sobersides, with her dull sleepy glance, her grave slow walk, and dignified, prudish airs; who could ever think that once she was the blue-eyed, whirling, scampering, head-over-heels, mad little firework that we call a kitten.

What marvellous vitality a kitten has. It is really something very beautiful the way life bubbles over in the little creatures. They rush about, and mew, and spring; dance on their hind legs, embrace everything with their front ones, roll over and over and over, lie on their backs and kick.

Jerome K Jerome (1859–1927), writer and humourist

The kitten sleeps upon the hearth,
The crickets long have ceased their mirth;

There's nothing stirring in the house
Save one 'wee', hungry, nibbling mouse . . .

🐾 **Dorothy Wordsworth**, 'The Cottager to her Infant', 1805

It is a very inconvenient habit of kittens (Alice had once made the remark) that, whatever you say to them, they always purr. 'If they would only purr for "yes" and mew for "no", or any rule of that sort,' she had said, 'so that one could keep up a conversation! But how *can* you talk with a person if they always say the same thing?'

🐾 **Lewis Carroll** *(Charles Lutwidge Dodgson)*, 'Alice Through the Looking Glass', 1871

The playful kitten, with its pretty little tigerish gambols, is infinitely more amusing than half the people one is obliged to live within the world.

🐾 **Lady Morgan** *(1783–1859)*, author

But kicking and beating and staring and that,
I have borne with the spirit becoming a cat:
There was but one thing which I could not sustain,
So great was my sorrow, so hopeless my pain.

One morning, laid safe in a warm little bed,
That down in the stable I'd carefully spread,
Three sweet little kittens as ever you saw,
I hid, as I thought, in some trusses of straw.

I was never so happy, I think, nor so proud
I mewed to my kittens and purred out aloud,
And thought with delight of the merry carousing
We'd have, when I first took them with me a-mousing.

But how shall I tell you the sorrowful ditty?
I'm sure it would melt even Growler to pity;
For the very next morning my darlings I found
Lying dead by the horse pond, all mangled and
    drowned.

Poor darlings, I dragged them along to the stable,
And did all to warm them a mother was able;

But, alas, all my licking and mewing were vain,
And I thought I should never be happy again.

🐾 *Ann Taylor* (1782–1866), 'The Last Dying
Speech and Confession of Poor Puss'

No one who has carefully and kindly brought up a
kitten from its birth, could fail to find it first a
charming playmate and then a firm friend. But it
must be very gently and kindly treated, from the time
when it makes its first excursion from its mother's
basket, and long before it has any other food than its
mother's milk. It must be taught to know that a hand
is a kind thing. My pussies learn this for their first
lesson and never forget it . . .

Tommy is my latest pet, and promises to be a
handsome and charming addition to our pussy folk.
He is with me in the mornings when I open my
letters, and is the one who has most appreciation of
the many trade circulars brought by the early post.
Most of them are printed on thin crackly paper, and
when loosely crushed in the hand they make nice

balls that he butts and tosses and chases all over the room. Or if I throw them into the wastepaper basket, he jumps on its edge, and tips it over and hunts out its ample contents for liberal distribution about the floor. And when we have the usual pussy-parade on the lawn at about seven on summer evenings; when, in turn with the bigger ones, he has had some good runs and jumps at the feather on the end of a whip which is the orthodox plaything, in pure delight of frisk and frolic he executes a *pas seul* on his own account, making a rapid series of monkey-jumps with high-arched back an helm hard a-port.

I know all my pussies in the dark not only by the feel of their coats, but by the different tone and quality of their purr. A kitten's purr is rather hard and rattly, high-pitched and unmelodious.

🐾 **Gertrude Jekyll** *(1843–1932)*, garden designer and writer

Buds will be roses and kittens, cats – more's the pity.

🐾 **Louisa May Alcott** (1832–1888), novelist

A dark November night. Late. The back door wide.
Beyond the doorway, the step off into space.
On the threshold, looking out,
With foxy furry tail lifted, a kitten.
Somewhere out there a badger, our lodger,
A stripe-faced rusher at cats, a grim savager,
Is crunching the bones and meat of a hare
That I left out for her twilight emergence
From under the outhouses.
The kitten flirts its tail, arches its back,
All its hairs are inquisitive.
Dare I go for a pee?
Something is moving there – just in dark.
A prowling lump. A tabby Tom. Grows.
And the battered master of the house
After a month at sea, comes through the doorway,
Recovered from his nearly fatal mauling,
Two probably three pounds heavier
Since that last appearance
When he brought in his remains to die or be
    doctored.
He deigns to recognise me,
With his criminal eyes, his deformed voice.

Then poises, head lowered, muscle-bound,
Like a bull for the judges,
A thick Devon bull,
Sniffing the celebration of sardines.

🐾 *Ted Hughes* (1930–1998), poet, 'Pets'

He was the funniest, tiniest kitten imaginable, with a
little round head, an innocent and baby-like expression
of countenance, and short uncertain legs that always
bore him diagonally and broke down three or for times
in carrying their owner for a yard, and with a short
pointed tail that stuck out straight behind him when he
sat in front of the fire . . . Beautiful creature as he is
now, looking a very monarch among cats as he walks
majestically on the lawn or lies tiger-like in his favourite
nest of long grass, I cherish a very kindly remembrance
of the days when he was so little and so wicked, and
occasionally find myself wishing that he had remained
about the size of a moderate rat, and retained the very
quaint and eccentric gambols of his early youth . . .

🐾 *Rev. John G. Wood*, 'Petland Revisited', 1890

Our office cat is a happy cat
She has had two hundred kittens
And every one has been adopted into happy homes
By our cat-loving Britons.

🐾 **Stevie Smith** *(1902–1971)*, 'Our Office Cat'

I learn the lesson of life from a little kitten of mine, one of two. The old cat comes in and says, very cross, 'I didn't ask you in here, I like to have my Missis to myself!' And he runs at them. The bigger and handsomer kitten runs away, but the littler one *stands her ground*, and when the old enemy comes near enough kisses his nose, and makes the peace. That is the lesson of life, to kiss one's enemy's nose, always standing one's ground . . .

🐾 **Florence Nightingale**, Letter to Norman Bonham Carter, 1895

Last May Day my cat gave birth
To six enchanting little kittens,
May kittens, all white with little black tails.
It certainly was a delightful nursery basket.
The cook, however, – for cooks are cruel
And human kindness never flourishes in a kitchen –
Wanted to drown five of the six.
Five white, black-tailed kittens
This wretched woman wanted to murder!
I soon saw to her! May heaven bless
My human kindness! The dear kittens
Grew and soon they were parading
With their tails in the air through the house
    and yard.
And in spite of the cook's fiercest looks
They grew and practised their little voices
Outside her window at night.
And I, watching them grow like that,
I praised myself and my humanity.
One year has passed and the kittens are now cats
And it is May Day! How shall I describe
The spectacle before me!
Throughout the house, from cellar to attic,

In every corner here is a nursery!
Here is the one, and there the other little cat,
In cupboards, baskets, under tables, under stairs,
Even the old one – I hardly dare say it! –
Is in the cook's virginal bed.
And each, yes, each of the seven cats,
Has seven, – would you believe it! – seven kittens,
May kittens, all white with black tails!
The cook is furious; I fail to dampen
The blind rage of this woman;
She wants to drown all forty nine!
And I – oh dear, my head is spinning –
Oh, human kindness, how will I safeguard you!
What shall I do with fifty six cats!

🐾 *Theodor Storm* *(1817–1888)*, poet and novelist

Few animals exhibit more maternal tenderness, or
show a greater love for their offspring, than the cat.

🐾 *Rev. W. Bingley*, 'Animal Biography', 1829

We remember being much amused with seeing a kitten manifestly making a series of experiments upon the patience of its mother – trying how far the latter would put up with positive bites and thumps. The kitten ran at her every moment, gave her a knock or a bite of the tail; and then ran back again, to recommence the assault. The mother sat looking at her, as if betwixt tolerance and admiration, to see how far the spirit of the family was inherited or improved by her sprightly offspring. At length, however, the 'little Pickle' presumed too far, and the mother, lifting up her paw, and meeting her at the very nick of the moment, gave her one of the most unsophisticated boxes of the ear we ever beheld. It send her rolling half over the room, and made her com to a most ludicrous pause, with the oddest little look of premature and wincing meditation.

🐾 *Leigh Hunt* *(1784–1859)*, essayist and poet

The most skittish kittens usually make the best cats. The cat is an animal of naturally a very strong will, being most impatient of control, and the kitten that is allowed quietly to enjoy unmolested freedom of purpose in its queer little ways and freaks will develop, under good treatment, into a noble-spirited and well-behaved cat.

🐾 *Philip M. Rule*, 'The Cat', 1887

Chapter Three

Cats At Home

A house without a cat, and a well-fed, well-petted, and properly revered cat, may be a perfect house, perhaps, but how can it prove its title? If a house is to be a home, it needs a cat.

🐾 *Mark Twain* *(Samuel Langhorne Clemens)*
(1835–1910), novelist

Every one is aware that a perfectly comfortable, well-fed cat will occasionally come to his house and settle there, deserting a family by whom it is lamented, and to whom it could, if it chose, find its way back with ease. This conduct is a mystery which may lead us to infer that cats form a great secret society, and that they come and go in pursuance of some policy connected with education, or perhaps with witchcraft.

We have known a cat to abandon his home for years.
Once in six months he would return and look about
him with an air of some contempt. 'Such,' he seemed
to say, 'were my humble beginnings.'

🐾 *Andrew Lang* *(1844–1912)*, essayist and author

I am the Cat. And you lie!
I am the Atheist!
All laws
I coldly despise.
I have yellow eyes,
I am the Cat on the Mat the child draws
When it first has a pencil to use.
I muse
Over the hearth with my 'minishing eyes
Until after
The last coal dies.
Every tunnel of the mouse,
Every channel of the cricket,
I have smelt.
I have felt

The secret shifting of the mouldered rafter,
And heard
Every bird in the thicket . . .
I, born of a race of strange things,
Of deserts, great temples, great kings,
In the hot sands where the nightingale never sings!
Old he-gods of ingle and hearth,
Young she-gods of fur and silk –
Not mud of the earth –
Are the things I dream of.

🐾 **Ford Madox Ford** *(1873–1939)*, 'The Cat
of the House'

If the cat waits for long hours, silent beside the crack
of the wainscot, it is for pure pleasure. Cats do not
keep mice away; it is my belief that they preserve
them for the chase.

🐾 **Oswald Barron** *(1868–1939)*, author and
antiquary

As cat a good mouser, is needful in house,
Because for her commons she killeth the mouse;
So ravening curs, as many do keep,
Makes master want meat, and his dog to kill sheep.

Thomas Tusser, 'Five Hundred Points of
   Good Husbandry', 1557

For my own part, I am excluded all conversation with
animals that delight only in a country life, and am
therefore forced to entertain myself as well as I can
with my little dog and cat. They both of them sit by
my fire every night, expecting my coming home with
impatience; and at my entrance, never fail of running
up to me, and bidding me welcome, each of them in
his proper language. As they have been bred up
together from their infancy, and seen no other
company, they have learned each other's manners, so
that the dog often gives himself the airs of a cat, and
the cat, in several of her motions and gestures, affects
the behaviour of the little dog. When they are at
play, I often make one with them; and sometimes

please myself with considering, how much reason and instinct are capable of delighting each other.

🐾 *Richard Steele* *(1672–1729)*, essayist

All that matters is to be at one with the living God
To be a creature in the house of the God of Life.

Like a cat asleep on a chair,
At peace, in peace
And at one with the master of the house, with the
   mistress,
At home, at home in the house of the living,
Sleeping on the hearth, and yawning before the fire.

Sleeping on the hearth of the living world
Yawning at home before the fire of life
Feeling the presence of the living God
Like a great reassurance
A deep calm in the heart
A presence
As of the master sitting at the board

In his own and greater being,
In the house of life.

🐾 *D. H. Lawrence* (1885–1930), 'Pax'

A catless couple had lately come to live next door. He
determined to adopt them . . . Meanwhile its own
family were seeking for it high and low. They had
not cared overmuch about it while they had it; now it
was gone they were inconsolable . . .

At the end of a fortnight the cat, finding he had
not, after all, bettered himself, came back. The family
were so surprised that at first they could not be sure
whether he was flesh and blood, or a spirit come to
comfort them. After watching him eat half a pound
of raw steak, they decided he was material, and
caught him up and hugged him to their bosoms. For
a week they overfed him and made much of him.
Then the excitement cooling, he found himself
dropping back into his old position, and didn't like it,
and went next door again.

The next door people had also missed him, and

they likewise greeted his return with extravagant ebullitions of joy. This gave the cat an idea. He saw that his game was to play the two families off one against the other; which he did. He spent an alternate fortnight with each, and lived like a fighting cock. His return was always greeted with enthusiasm, and every means were adopted to induce him to stay. His little whims were carefully studied, his favourite dishes kept in constant readiness.

The destination of his goings leaked out at length, and then the two families quarrelled about him over the fence.

🐾 *Jerome K Jerome* *(1859–1927)*, author and humourist

A blazing fire, a warm rug, candles lit and curtains drawn, the kettle on for tea, . . . and finally the cat before you, attracting your attention – it is a scene which everybody likes unless he has a morbid aversion to cats; which is not common . . . The cat purrs, as if it applauded our consideration, – and gently moves its tail. What an odd expression of the power to be irritable and the will to be pleased there is in its face. We must own, that we do not prefer a cat in the act of purring, or of looking in that manner. It reminds us of the sort of smile, or simmer (simper is too weak and fleeting a word) that is apt to be in the faces of irritable people when they are pleased to be a state of satisfaction. We prefer, for a general expression, the cat in a quiet, unpretending state . . .

Poor Pussy! She looks up at us again . . . and symbolically gives a twist of a yawn and a lick to her whiskers. Now she proceeds to clean herself all over, having a just sense of the demands of her elegant person, – beginning judiciously with her paws, and fetching amazing tongues at her hind-hips. Anon, she scratches her neck with a foot of rapid delight, leaning her head towards it, and shutting her eyes, half to accommodate the action of the skin and half to enjoy the luxury. She then rewards her paws with a few more touches; – look at the action of her head and neck, how pleasing it is, the ears pointed forward, and the neck gently arching to and fro.

Finally she gives a sneeze, and another twist of mouth and whiskers, and then, curling her tail towards her front claws, settles herself on her hind quarters in an attitude of bland meditation.

What does she think of? – of her saucer of milk at breakfast? or of the thump she got yesterday in the kitchen for stealing the meat? or of her own meat, the Tartar's dish, noble horseflesh? or of her friend the cat next door, the most impassioned of serenaders? or of her little ones, some of whom are now large, and all of them gone? Is *that* among her recollections when she looks pensive? Does she taste of the noble prerogative-sorrows of man? . . .

Cats at firesides live luxuriously, and are the picture of comfort; but lest they should not bear their portion of trouble in this world, they have the drawbacks of being liable to be shut out of doors on cold nights, beatings from the 'aggravated' cooks, overpettings of children (how should we like to be squeezed and pulled about in that manner by some patronising giants?) and last but not least, horrible merciless tramples of unconscious human feet and the unfeeling legs of chairs. Elegance, comfort, and security seem the order of the day on all sides, and you are going to sit down to dinner, or to music, or to take tea, when all of a sudden, the cat gives a squall as if she was mashed; and you are not sure the fact is otherwise. Yet she gets in the way again, as before; and dares all the feet and mahogany in the room. Beautiful present sufficingness of a cat's imagination! Confined to the snug circle of her own sides, and the two next inches of rug or carpet.

🐾 *Leigh Hunt* (1784–1859), poet and writer

Dearest cat, honoured guest of my old house,
Arch your supple, tingling back,
And curl upon my knee, to let me
Bathe my fingers in your warm fur.

Green eyes half closed mock me as they caress,
After a slow, luxurious shudder.
Gold flecked and drowsy, your eyes
Watch me ironic, yet benign.

Not for you, my philosophic old friend,
The blind devotion of a boisterous dog,
Yet my heart tells me that you love me still.

Your fleeting though understanding love
Satisfies me; and in you, serene thinker, I hail
Two subtler qualities – softness and doubt.

🐾 *François Lemaître* (1853–1914), poet and
    dramatist

A cat rolled up into a ball, or crouched with its paws
folded underneath it, seems an emblem of repose and
contentment. There is something soothing in the
mere sight of it.

🐾 *Charles Ross*, 'The Book of Cats', 1868

He liked companionship, but he wouldn't be petted,
or fussed over, or sit in anyone's lap a moment; he
always extricated himself from such familiarity with

dignity and with no show of temper. If there was any petting to be done, however, he chose to do it. Often he would sit looking at me, and then, moved by a delicate affection, come and pull at my coat and sleeve until he could touch my face with his nose, and then go away contented.

🐾 *Charles Dudley Warner* (1829–1900),
  essayist and novelist

When the tea is brought at five o'clock,
And all the neat curtains are drawn with care,
The little black cat with bright green eyes
Is suddenly purring there.

At first she pretends, having nothing to do,
She has come in merely to blink by the grate,
But, though tea may be late or the milk may be sour,
She is never late.

And presently her agate eyes
Take a soft large milky haze,

And her independent casual glance
Becomes a stiff hard gaze.

Then she stamps her claws or lifts her ears,
Or twists her tail and begins to stir,
Till suddenly all her lithe body becomes
One breathing trembling purr.

The children eat and wriggle and laugh;
The two old ladies stroke their silk:
But the cat is grown small and thin with desire,
Transformed to a creeping lust for milk.

The white saucer like some full moon descends
At last from the clouds of the table above;
She sighs and dreams and thrills and glows,
Transfigured with love.

She nestles over the shining rim,
Buries her chin in the creamy sea;
Her tail hangs loose; each drowsy paw
Is doubled under each bending knee.

A long dim ecstasy holds her life;
Her world is an infinite shapeless white,
Till her tongue has curled the last holy drop,
Then she sinks back into the night,

Draws and dips her body to heap
Her sleepy nerves in the great arm-chair,
Lies defeated and buried deep
Three or four hours unconscious there.

🐾 **Harold Monro** (1879–1932), 'Milk for the Cat'

I have often felt the benefit, after a long spell of mental effort, of having my cat sitting across my shoulders.

🐾 **Louis Wain** (1860–1939), artist and illustrator

The nature of this beast is, to love the place of her breeding, neither will she tarry in any strange place, although carried far, being never willing to forsake the house, for the love of any man, and most contrary to the nature of a dog who will travel abroad with his master. They love fire and warm places, whereby it often falleth out that they often burn their coats. It is needless to spend any time about her loving nature to man, how she flattereth by rubbing her skin against one's legs, how she whurleth with her voice, having as many tunes as turns, for she hath one voice to beg and to complain, another to testify her delight and pleasure, another among her own kind by flattering, by hissing, by puffing, by spitting, in so much as some have thought that they have a peculiar intelligible language among themselves. Therefore how she beggeth, playeth, leapeth, looketh, catcheth, fosseth with her foot, riseth up to strings held over her head, sometimes creeping, sometimes lying on her back, playing with one foot, sometime on her belly, snatching now with mouth, and anon with foot, apprehending greedily anything save the hand of a man, with diverse such gestical actions, it is needless to stand upon; in so much as Caelius was wont to say, that being free from his studies and more urgent weighty affairs, he was not ashamed to play and sport himself with his cat, and verily it may be called an idle man's pastime.

 *Edward Topsell*, 'The History of Four-Footed Beasts', 1607

As I mused by the hearthside,
Puss said to me:
'There burns the Fire, man,
And here sit we.

'Four Walls around us
    Against the cold air;
And the latchet drawn close
    To the draughty Stair.

'A Roof o'er our heads
    Star-proof, moon immune,
And a wind in the chimney
    To wail us a tune.

'What Felicity!' miaowed he,
    'Where none may intrude;
Just Man and Beast – met
    In this Solitude!

'Dear God, what security,
    Comfort and bliss!
And to think, too, what ages
    Have brought us to this!

'You in your sheep's-wool coat,
    Buttons of bone,
And me in my fur-about
    On the warm hearthstone.'

🐾 *Walter De La Mare* (1873–1956), 'Comfort'

We may learn some useful lessons from cats, as
indeed, from all animals . . . Cats may teach us
patience and perseverance, and earnest concentration
of mind on a desired object, as they watch for hours
together by a mouse-hole, or in ambush for a bird . . .

In their delicate walking amidst the fragile articles on a table or mantelpiece is illustrated the tact and discrimination by which we should thread rather than force our way; and, in pursuit of our own ends, avoid the injuring of others. In their noiseless tread and stealthy movements, we are reminded of the frequent importance of secrecy and caution prior to action, while their promptitude at the right moment, warns us, on the other hand, against the evils of irresolution and delay . . . As your Cat rubs her head against something you offer her, which she either does not fancy or does not want, she instructs you that there is a gracious mode of refusing a thing; and as she sits up like a bear, on her hind legs, to ask for something (which Cats will often do for a long time together), you may see the advantage of a winning and engaging way, as well when you are seeking a favour as when you think fit to decline one . . . A cat rolled up into a ball, or crouched with its paws folded underneath it, seems an emblem of repose and contentment. There is something soothing in the mere sight of it.

🐾 *Anonymous,* 'The Book of Cats', 1868

Cats, like men, are flatterers.

Walter Savage Landor *(1775–1864)*, poet
and writer

MY pipe is lit, my grog is mixed,
My curtains drawn and all is snug;
Old Puss is in her elbow-chair,
And Tray is sitting on the rug.
Last night I had a curious dream,
Miss Susan Bates was Mistress Mogg, –
What d'ye think of that, my cat?
What d'ye think of that, my dog?

She looked so fair, she sang so well,
I could but woo and she was won,
Myself in blue, the bride in white,
The ring was placed, the deed was done!
Away we went in chaise-and-four,
As fast as grinning boys could flog,
What d'ye think of that, my cat?
What d'ye think of that, my dog?

My Susan's taste was superfine,
As proved by bills that had no end;
I never had a decent coat,
I never had a coin to spend!
She forced me to resign my club,
Lay down my pipe, retrench my grog, –
What d'ye think of that, my cat?
What d'ye think of that, my dog?

Now was not that an awful dream
For one who single is and snug,
With Pussy in the elbow-chair
And Tray reposing on the rug? –
If I must totter down the hill,
'Tis safest done without a clog, –
What d'ye think of that, my cat?
What d'ye think of that, my dog?

Thomas Hood (1799–1845), comic poet

Dearest Sylvia,

Can you explain how and why cats make love to
us? Tiber will come, if I am reading or writing or

lying on my bed and will 'tease tow' with his claws. Then coming closer, will gaze into my face, suddenly dig his pointed muzzle under my chin once or twice, retreat, roll on his side, inviting my hand, turn his head dreamily to one side, passive and luxurious. Then he will turn on me almost fiercely with a burst of purring, and so on, and so on.

But is this, as I think, reserved for human lovers? With a female cat I think he displays no such graces but is fiercely practical. It is more like the love that was shown him by his mother when he was a kitten. And naturally it is shown most strongly before and after I have fed him. But the luxury of his furry love is very beautiful . . .

:: **David Garnett**, Letter to Sylvia Townsend Warner, 1973

Dearest David,

Tiber makes love to you for the good reason that he loves you, and loves making love. Cats are passionate and voluptuous, they get satisfaction from mating but no pleasure (the females dislike it, and this is wounding to the male), no voluptuous-ness; *and no appreciation*. Tiber has the pleasure of being pleased and knowing he pleases in his love-making with you. I am so glad you have each other. Does he roll on his head? Does he fall asleep with an ownerly paw laid over you?

We had a dark grey cat (Norfolk bred, very Norfolk in character) called Tom. He was reserved, domineering, voluptuous – much as I imagine Tiber to be. When he was middle-aged, he gave up nocturnal prowlings and slept on my bed, against my feet. One evening I was reading in bed when I became aware that Tom was staring at me. I put down my book, said nothing, watched. Slowly, with a look of intense concentraton, he got up and advanced on me, like Tarquin with ravishing strides, poised himself, put out a front paw, and stroked my cheek as I used to stroke his chops. A human caress from a cat. I felt very meagre and ill-educated that I could not purr . . .

🐾 **Sylvia Townsend Warner**, Letter to David Garnett, 1973

The white cat furies
In a squirm of purring.

He writhes in his delight,
Rolling his restless head
He tunnels my ready lap.

He loops his length
Hooping his lithe spine.

The white cat settles,
Licks at a stiffened leg,
Then sleeps – a lazy shape.

The white cat dreams of snow fields,
The small musical pipes of birds,
Licking his lips in sleep.

🐾 *Gerard Benson*, 'Duffy'

Presumption is our natural and original infirmity. Of
all creatures man is the most miserable and frail, and
therewithal the proudest and disdainfullest . . . It is

through the vanity of the same imagination that he dare equal himself to God, that he ascribeth divine conditions unto himself, that he selecteth and separateth himself from out the rank of other creatures . . . How knoweth he by the virtue of his understanding the inward and secret motions of beasts? By what comparison from them to us doth he conclude the brutishness he ascribeth unto them? When I am playing with my cat, who knows whether she have more sport in dallying with me than I have in gaming with her? We entertain one another with mutual apish tricks. If I have my hour to begin or to refuse, so hath she hers.

🐾 *Michel Montaigne* (1533–1592), essayist

It is not only by gesture that cats express their feelings. Besides their hideous nocturnal howls, cats give expression to their desires by gentle sounds. Almost everyone must have met with a cat which by mewing expressed its wish for a door to be opened, or which thus begged for a little milk. Cats then have a language of their own made up of sounds and gestures. Cats also have a will of their own, as all must know who have tried to retain on the lap, a cat minded to go elsewhere, or who have observed the determination with which they pursue the objects of their desires.

🐾 **St George Mivart**, 'The Cat', 1881

The extraordinary patience with which a cat will watch a mouse-hole, for hours, is, no doubt, a natural propensity. This determined bending of the will to one object, is, probably, a principle cause of the fascination that some serpents possess. One of the most remarkable properties of a domestic cat is the anxiety with which it makes itself acquainted, not only with every part of its usual habitation but with the dimensions and external qualities of every object by which it is surrounded. Cats do not very readily adapt themselves to a change of houses; but we have watched the process by which one, whose attachment to a family is considerable, reconciles itself to such a change. He surveys every room in the house, from the garret to the cellar; if the door is shut, he waits till it be opened to complete the survey; he ascertains the relative size and position of every article of furniture; and when he has acquired this knowledge, he sits down contented with his new situation.

🐾 *James Rennie, William Ogilvy and Charles Knight*, 'The Menageries: Quadrupeds', 1829

If I might alter kind,
What, think you, I would be?
Nor fish, nor fowl, nor flea, nor frog
Nor squirrel on the tree;
The fish the hook, the fowl
The liméd twig doth catch,
The flea the finger, and the frog
The bustard doth dispatch.
The squirrel thinking nought,
That featly cracks the nut;
The greedy goshawk wanting prey

In dread of death doth put;
But scorning all these kinds,
I would become a cat,
To combat with the creeping mouse,
And scratch the screeking rat.

I would be present, aye,
And at my lady's call;
To guard her from the fearful mouse,
In parlour and in hall;
In kitchen, for his life,
He should not show his head;
The pear in poke should lie untouched
When she were gone to bed.
The mouse should stand in fear,
So should the squeaking rat;
And this would I do if I were
Converted to a cat.

George Turberville *(1540–1610)*,
    'The Lover Whose Mistress Feared a Mouse'

Never were two creatures better together than a dog
and a cat brought up in the same house from a whelp
and a kitten; so kind, so gamesome and diverting,
that it was half the entertainment of the family to see
the gambols and love-tricks that passed betwixt them.
Only it was observed, that still at meal-times, when
scraps fell from the table, or a bone was thrown at
them, they would be snarling and spitting at one
another under the table like the worst of foes.

🐾 **Samuel Croxall**, 'Fables of Aesop and
  Others', 1797

Now old Mr Johnson had some troubles of his own,
He had a yellow cat that just wouldn't leave his home,
He tried and he tried to give the cat away,
He gave it to a man going far far away.

But the cat came back the very next day,
The cat came back, we thought he was a goner,
The cat came back, he just wouldn't stay away.

But the cat came back he wouldn't stay away,
He was sitting on the porch the very next day.

🐾 *Harry S. Miller*, 'And the Cat came back',
    1883

In the case of those domestic animals, which are
honorific and are reputed beautiful, there is a
subsidiary basis of merit that should be spoken of.
Apart from the birds which belong in the honorific
class of domestic animals, and which owe their place
in this class to their non-lucrative character alone, the
animals which merit particular attention are cats, dogs,
and fast horses. The cat is less reputable than the other
two just named, because she is less wasteful; she may
even serve a useful purpose. She lives with man on
terms of equality, knows nothing of that relation of
status which is the ancient basis of all distinctions of
worth, honor, and repute, and she does not lend
herself with facility to an invidious comparison
between her own and his neighbors. The exception to
this last rule occurs in the case of such scarce and

fanciful products as the Angora cat, which have some
slight honorific value on the ground of expensiveness.

🐾 *Thorstein Veblen*, 'The Theory of the
Leisure Class', 1899

The beggar's dog and widow's cat,
Feed thee, and thou wilt grow fat.

🐾 *William Blake* (1757–1827), poet, artist and
visionary

The cat you sent me . . . is certainly the most beautiful
and jolliest cat that e'er was seen . . . I can only say,
that 'tis very hard to keep him in, and that of a cat
brought up in religion, he is the most uneasy to be
confined to a cloister. He can never see a window open,
but immediately he is jumping out of it; he had ere this
leaped twenty times over the walls, had he not been
prevented; and there is no secular cat in Christendom
that is more a libertine, or more head-strong than he. I

am in hopes, however, that I shall persuade him to stay by the kind entertainment I give him; for I treat him with nothing but good cheese and Naples biscuits . . . He begins to grow tame already; yesterday I thought verily that he had torn off one of my hands in his wanton addresses. 'Tis doubtless one of the most playful creatures in the world; there's neither man, woman nor child, in my lodgings, that wears not some mark of his favour. But however lovely he is in his own person, it shall always be for your sake that I esteem him; and I shall love him so well, for the love I have for you, that I hope to give occasion to alter the proverb, and there hereafter it shall be said, *Who loves me, Loves my cat.*

🐾 **Vincent Voiture** *(1598–1648)*, Letter to a Lady Abbess

Better feed one cat than many mice.

🐾 *Anonymous*

January: A cottage evening.

The shutter closed, the lamp alight,
The faggot shopped and blazing bright,
The shepherd from his labour free
Dancing his children on his knee
Or toasting sloe boughs sputtering ripe
Or smoking glad his puthering pipe
While underneath his master's seat
The tired dog lies in slumbers sweet
Startling and whimpering in his sleep
Chasing still the straying sheep.
The cat rolled round in vacant chair
Or leaping children's knees to lair
Or purring on the warmer hearth
Sweet chorus to the crickets' mirth . . .
The housewife busy night and day
Cleareth the supper things away
While jumping cat starts from her seat
And streaking up on weary feet
The dog wakes at the welcome tones
That calls him up to pick the bones.

February: A thaw.

No more behind his master's heels
The dog creeps o'er his winter pace
But cocks his tail and o'er the fields
Runs many a wild and random chase
Following in spite of chiding calls
The startled cat wi' harmless glee
Scaring her up the weed green walls
Or mossy mottled apple tree.

🐾 *John Clare* (1793–1864), poet

'Yes,' said that lady, 'such lace cannot be got now for
either love or money . . . I always wash it myself.
And once it had a narrow escape. Of course, your
ladyship knows that such lace must never be starched
or ironed. Some people wash it in sugar and water,
and some in coffee, to make it the right yellow
colour; but I myself have a very good receipt for
washing it in milk, which stiffens it enough, and
gives it a very good creamy colour. Well, ma'am, I
had tacked it together (and the beauty of this fine

lace is that, when it is wet, it goes into a very little space), and put it to soak in milk, when, unfortunately, I left the room; on my return I found pussy on the table looking very like a thief, but gulping very uncomfortably, as if she was half-choked with something she wanted to swallow and could not. And, would you believe it? At first I pitied her, and said "Poor pussy! Poor pussy!" till, all at once, I looked and saw the cup of milk empty – cleaned out! "You naughty cat!" said I, and I believe I was provoked enough to give her a slap, which did no good, but only helped the lace down – just as one slaps a choking child on the back. I could have cried, I was so vexed; but I determined I would not give up the lace without a struggle for it. I hoped the lace might disagree with her, at any rate; but it would have been too much for Job, if he had seen, as I did, that cat come in, quite placid and purring, not a quarter of an hour after, and almost expecting to be stroked. "No, pussy!" said I, "if you have any conscience you ought not to expect that!" And then a thought struck me; and I rang the bell for my maid, and sent her to Mr Hoggins, with my compliments, and would he be kind enough to lend me one of his top-boots for an hour? I did not think there was anything odd in the message; but Jenny said the young men in the surgery laughed as if they would be ill at my wanting a top-boot. When it came, Jenny and I put pussy in, with her forefeet straight down, so that they were fastened, and could not scratch, and we gave her a teaspoonful of currant jelly in which (your ladyship must excuse me) I had mixed some tartar emetic. I shall never forget how anxious I was for the next half-hour. I took pussy to my own room, and spread a clean towel on the floor. I could have kissed her when she returned the lace to sight, very much as it had gone down. Jenny had boiling water ready, and we soaked it and soaked it, and spread it on a lavender bush in the sun before I could touch it again, even to put it in milk. But now your ladyship would never guess that it had been in pussy's inside.'

🐾 *Elizabeth Gaskell*, 'Cranford', 1853

The dog lies in his kennel,
And puss purrs on the rug,
And baby perches on my knee
For me to love and hug.

Pat the dog and stroke the cat,
Each in its degree;
And cuddle and kiss my baby,
And baby kiss me.

🐾 **Christina Rosetti** *(1830–1894)*, poet

I am, indeed, fully alive to the pleasure of being
invited out for a walk with a dog . . . But there is a
still greater charm, a more refined pleasure in the
company of a cat, whose good pleasure it is to lead
his master. The cat does not invite one out for a
walk; it does not experience the ambulatory enjoyment peculiar to the dog; or at least it does not
appear to do so. It follows the person for whom it
has an affection, but always on condition that the
walk shall be a short one, and in a quiet place. A

thoughtful person who walks in the pleached alleys of an old fashioned garden, meditatively, book in hand, is particularly agreeable to the refined and delicate animal. Before such a one the cat will run, stop suddenly, and roll himself upon the gravelled path, rubbing his back against it with delight. There he will wait until his master comes up and caresses him, and then start off to go through the same 'high jinks' twenty paces farther on.

🐾 *Champfleury* *(Jules Fleury-Husson)*, 'The Cat Past and Present', 1885

Have I not sat with thee full many a night,
When dying embers were our only light,
When every creature did in slumbers lie,
Besides our cat, my Colin Clout and I?
No troublous thoughts the cat or Colin move,
While I alone am kept awake by love . . .

🐾 *John Gay*, 'The Shepherd's Week', 1714

Chapter Four

Nonsense And Nursery Cats

Dogs wander in and out of nursery rhymes
but are obviously ill at ease.
For cats this is home ground
    – a place of high jinks and clever silliness,
    – a place of mystery and magic
A place to pretend.

🐾 *Pam Brown*, living author

Pussy sits by the fire.
How can she be fair?
In walks little doggy,
'Pussy, are you there?
How d'ye do, Mistress Pussy?
Mistress Pussy, how d'ye do?'

'I thank you kindly, little dog,
I fare as well as you.'

🐾 *Anonymous*

Dame Trot and her cat
Led a peaceable life
When they were not troubled
With other folks' strife.

When Dame had her dinner
Pussy would wait
And was sure to receive
A nice piece from her plate.

Old Dame Trot
Going to the fair
With the cat on her shoulder
To see the folks there.

She went to buy apples,
And sugar and spice,

While Pussy at home
Was to catch all the mice.

But I'm sorry to say,
This pet of the cats,
Stead of killing the mice,
Was fiddling to rats.

She went for some ale,
Because she was dry,
When she came back,
Puss was making a pie.

She went out to buy her
A bonnet or hat,
When she came back
Puss was killing a rat.

She trotted once more
For brandy and wine
When she came back
Puss had sat down to dine.

Dame Trot and her cat
Sat down for a chat.
The Dame sat on this side,
The Puss sat on that.

'Puss,' says the Dame,
'Can you catch a rat?
Or a mouse in the dark?'
'Purr,' says the cat . . .

🐾 *Anonymous*

'Who's that ringing at my door bell?'
'I'm a little pussy-cat and I'm not very well.'
'Then rub your little nose with a little mutton fat,
And that's the best thing for a sick pussy cat.'

🐾 *D'Arcy Wentworth Thompson*, 'Nursery
Nonsense', 1864

Clarence was with me as concerned the revolution, but in a modified way. His idea was a republic, without privileged orders, but with a hereditary royal family at the head of it instead of an elective chief magistrate. He believed that no nation that had ever known the joy of worshiping a royal family could ever be robbed of it and not fade away and die of melancholy. I urged that kings were dangerous. He said, then have cats. He was sure that a royal family of cats would answer every purpose. They would be as useful as any other royal family, they would know as much, they would have the same virtues and the same treacheries, the same disposition to get up shindies with other royal cats, they would be laughably vain and absurd and never know it, they would be wholly inexpensive; finally, they would have as sound a divine right as any other royal house, and 'Tom VII., or Tom XI., or Tom XIV. by the grace of God King,' would sound as well as it would when applied to the ordinary royal tomcat with tights on. 'And as a rule,' said he, in his neat modern English, 'the character of these cats would be considerably above the character of the average king, and this would be an immense moral advantage to the nation, for the reason that a nation always models its morals after its monarch's. The worship of royalty being founded in unreason, these graceful and harmless cats would easily become as sacred as any other royalties, and indeed more so, because it would presently be noticed that they hanged nobody, beheaded nobody, imprisoned nobody, inflicted no cruelties or injustices of any sort, and so must be worthy of a deeper love and reverence than the customary human king, and would certainly get it. The eyes of the whole harried world would soon be fixed upon this humane and gentle system, and royal butchers would presently begin to disappear; their subjects would fill the vacancies with catlings from our own royal house; we should become a factory; we should supply the thrones of the world; within forty years all Europe would be governed by cats, and we should furnish the cats. The reign of universal peace would begin then, to end no more forever . . . Me-e-e-yow-ow-ow-ow – fzt! – wow!'

🐾 *Mark Twain* (Samuel Langhorne Clemens), 'A Connecticut Yankee in King Arthur's Court', 1889

What did she see – oh, what did she see,
As she stood learning against the tree?
Why all the Cats had come to tea.

What a fine turn out – from round about,
All the houses had let them out,
And here they were with a scamper and shout.

'Mew-mew-mew!' was all they could say,
And, 'We hope we find you well today.'

Oh, what should she do – oh, what should she do?
What a lot of milk they would get through;
For here they were with 'mew-mew-mew!'

She didn't know – Oh, she didn't know,
If bread and butter they'd like or no;
They might want little mice, oh! oh! oh!

Dear me – oh dear me,
All the cats had come to tea.

🐾 *Kate Greenaway* *(1846–1901),* 'The Cats
Have Come To Tea'

There was a wee bit mousikie,
That lived in Gilberaty-O,
It couldno' get a bite o' cheese,
For cheatie pussy-catty-O.

It said unto the cheeseky,
'Oh fain would I be at ye-O,
If 'twere no' for the cruel claws
Of cheatie pussy-catty-O.'

Anonymous

My cat may look like your cat
With know-it-all eyes like yours
Spreadeagling itself on your tummy
Before purring and sharpening its claws

My cat may look like your cat
With sticky-out whiskers like yours
And the knack of slipping off branches
To land safely each time on all-paws

My cat may sound like your cat
With a pitiful mew like yours
After scratching the arms of the sofa
Tries to burrow under closed doors

My cat may look like your cat
And my cat may sound like yours
But my cat plays the saxophone
And dances to wild applause.

🐾 **Roger McGough**, 'The Bee's Knees', 2003

Jack Spratt
Had a cat;
It had but one ear;
It went to buy butter
When butter was dear.

🐾 *Anonymous*

I love little pussy,
Her coat is so warm,
And if I don't hurt her,
She'll do me no harm.

I'll not pull her tail,
Nor drive her away,
But pussy and I
Very gently will play

And I'll sit by her side
And give her some food,
And pussy will love me
Because I am good.

🐾 *Anonymous*

Sitting at the window
In her cloak and hat,
I saw Mother Tabbyskins
The real old cat.

Very old, very old,
Crumpletey and lame;
Teaching kittens how to scold –
Is it not a shame?

Kittens in the garden,
Looking in her face,
Learning how to spit and swear –
Oh, what a disgrace!
    Very wrong, very wrong,
    Very wrong and bad;
    Such a subject for our song
    Makes us all too sad.

Old Mother Tabbyskins,
Sticking out her head,
Gave a howl and then a yowl,
Hobbled off to bed.
    Very sick, very sick,
    Very savage, too
    Pray, send for a doctor quick
    Any one will do.

Doctor Mouse came creeping,
Creeping to her bed,
Lanced her gums and felt her pulse,
Whispered she was dead.
    Very sly, very sly,
    The real old cat
    Open kept her weather eye,
    Mouse, beware of that!

Old Mother Tabbyskins,
Saying 'Serves him right!'
Gobbled up the doctor
With infinite delight.
    'Very fast, very fast,
    Very pleasant, too.
    What a pity it can't last.
    Send another, do.'

Doctor Dog comes running,
Just to see her begs.
Round his neck a comforter,
Trousers on his legs.

Very grand, very grand,
Golden headed cane
Swinging gaily from his hand,
Mischief in his brain.

'Dear Mother Tabbyskins,
And how are you now,
Let me feel your pulse, so-so,
Show your tongue, Bow-wow!'
    'Very sick, very sick!'
    'Please attempt to purr.
    Will you take a draught or pill,
    Which do you prefer?'

Doctor Dog comes nearer,
Says she must be bled.
I heard Mother Tabbyskins
Screaming in her bed.
    Very fast very fast
    Scuffling out and in,
    Doctor Dog looks full and queer
    Where is Tabbyskin?

I will tell the moral
Without any fuss:
Those who lead the young astray
Always suffer thus.
    Very nice, very nice
    Let our conduct be.
    For all doctors are not mice,
    Some are dogs, you see.

🐾 *Anonymous*

Ding, dong, bell; Pussy's in the well,
Who put her in? Little Tommy Green.
Who pulled her out? Little Tommy Stout.
What a naughty boy was that,
So to drown poor Pussy Cat.
Who ne'er did him any harm,
But killed all the mice in the farmer's barn.

🐾 *Anonymous*

Little Robin Redbreast sat upon a tree,
Up went Pussy-Cat, and down came he,
Down came Pussy-Cat, away Robin ran;
Says little Robin Redbreast: 'Catch me if you can!'

Little Robin Redbreast jumped upon a spade,
Pussy-cat jumped after him, and then he was afraid.
Little Robin chirped and sang, and what did Pussy say?
Pussy-cat said, 'Mew, mew, mew,' and Robin ran away.

🐾 *Anonymous*

There was a crooked man, and he went a crooked
    mile,
He found a crooked sixpence against a crooked stile.
He bought a crooked cat, which caught a crooked
    mouse,
And they all lived together in a little crooked house.

🐾 *Anonymous*

Three young rats with black felt hats,
Three young ducks with white straw flats,
Three young dogs with curling tails,
Three young cats with demi-veils,
Went out to walk with two young pigs
In satin vests and sorrel wigs.
But suddenly it chanced to rain
And so they all went home again.

🐾 *Anonymous*

Diddledy, Diddledy, Dumpty.
The cat ran up the plum tree.
I'll wager a crown,
I'll fetch you down.
Sing Diddledy, Diddledy, Dumpty.

🐾 *Anonymous*

Poussie, poussie, baudrons,
Where hae ye been?
I've been at London
To see the queen!

Poussie, poussie, baudrons,
What got ye there?
I got a guid fat mousikie
Rinning up a stair!

Poussie, poussie, baudrons,
What did ye do wi't?
I put it in my meal-pock,
To eat it to my bread!

🐾 *Anonymous*

It almost makes my cry to tell
What foolish Harriet befell.
Mamma and Nurse went out one day,
And left her all alone to play;
Now on the table close at hand

A box of matches chanced to stand;
And kind Mamma and Nurse had told her
That, if she touched them, they should scold her.
But Harriet said, 'Oh what a pity!
For when they burn it is so pretty;
They crackle so, and spit and flame;
Mamma, too, often does the same.'
    The pussy-cats heard this,
    And they began to hiss
    And stretch their claws and raise their paws,
    'Me-ow!' they said, 'Me-ow, me-o,
    You'll burn to death if you do so.'

But Harriet would not take advice,
She lit a match, it was so nice;
It crackled so, it burned so clear,
Exactly like the picture here.
She jumped for joy, and ran about
And was too pleased to put it out.
    The pussy-cats saw this
    And said, 'Oh naughty, naughty Miss!'
    And stretched their claws and raised their paws,
    'This is very, very wrong, you know!

Me-ow, me-o, me-ow, me-o,
You will be burned if you do so.'

And so! Oh! what a dreadful thing!
The fire has caught her apron string;
Her apron burns, her arms, her hair,
She burns all over everywhere.
    Then how the pussy-cats did mew,
    What else, poor pussies, could they do?
    They screamed for help, 'twas all in vain!
    So then they said, 'We'll scream again;
    Make haste, make haste, me-ow, me-o
    She'll burn to death, we told her so.'

So she was burnt with all her clothes,
And arms, and hair, and eyes, and nose,
Till she had nothing more to lose
Except her little scarlet shoes;
And nothing else but these was found
Among her ashes on the ground.
    And when the good cats sat beside
    The smoking ashes, how they cried!
    'Me-ow, me-oo, me-ow, me-oo,

What will Mamma and Nursey do?'
Their tears ran down their cheeks so fast
They made a little pond at last.

🐾 *Heinrich Hoffman*, 'Struwwelpeter', 1860

Pussie at the fireside
Suppin' up brose,
Doon came a cinder
And burnt pussy's nose.
'Och', said pussy,
'That's no fair'.
'Weel', said the cinder,
'Ye should'na been there'.

🐾 *Anonymous*

A cat came fiddling out of a barn
With a pair of bagpipes under her arm;
She could sing nothing but 'fiddle-cum-fee,
The mouse has married the bumble bee.'

Pipe, cat; dance, mouse;
We'll have a wedding at our good house.

🐾 *Anonymous*

Come dance a jig
To my granny's pig,
With a rowdy dowdy dowdy;
Come, dance a jig
To my granny's pig
And pussy-cat shall crowdy.

🐾 *Anonymous*

Pussy cat Mew jumped over a coal,
And in her best petticoat burnt a great hole.
Pussy cat Mew shall have no more milk,
Until her best petticoat's mended with silk.

🐾 *Anonymous*

Huff the talbot and our cat Tib
They took up sword and shield,
Tib for the red rose, Huff for the white,
To fight upon Bosworth Field.

Oh, it was dreary that night to bury
Those doughty warriors dead,
Under a white rose brave dog Huff,
And fierce Tib under a red.

Low lay Huff and long may he lie!
But our Tib took little harm:
He was up and away at dawn of day
With the rose-bush under his arm.

🐾 *Anonymous*, 'The War of the Roses'

In **A**dam's fall,
We sinned all.
Thy Life to mend,
This **B**ook attend.
The **C**at doth play,
And after slay.

🐾 *Victorian Alphabet*

D is for Dog,
Loyal, faithful and true.
I hope he gets married
To Pussy, don't you?

🐾 *Victorian Alphabet*

C stands for the Cats who live in your house,
They love milk and meat, but most a fat mouse.

🐾 *Victorian Alphabet*

Great **A**, little **a**,
Bouncing **B**;
The cat's in the cupboard
And she can't see me.

🐾 *Victorian Alphabet*

Two cats sat on a garden wall,
For an hour or so together;
First they talked about nothing at all,
And then they talked of the weather.
The first pussycat was a silly pussycat,
She had a wrapper to wrap her chin in.
But the second pussycat was sillier than that,
With her tail in a bag of linen.

🐾 *D'Arcy Wentworth Thompson*,
'Nursery Nonsense', 1864

The Owl and the Pussy-Cat went to sea
In a beautiful pea-green boat;
They took some honey, and plenty of money
Wrapped up in a five-pound note.
The Owl looked up to the moon above,
And sang to a small guitar:
'O lovely Pussy! O Pussy, my love!
What a beautiful Pussy you are, – you are,
What a beautiful Pussy you are!'

Pussy said to the owl: 'You elegant fowl!
How charmingly sweet you sing!
O let us be married – too long we have tarried –
But what shall we do for a ring?'
They sailed away for a year and a day
To the land where the Bong-tree grows,
And there in a wood, a Piggy-wig stood
With a ring in the end of his nose, – his nose,
With a ring in the end of his nose.

'Dear Pig, are you willing to sell for one shilling
Your ring?' Said the Piggy, 'I will.'
So they took it away, and were married next day

By the turkey who lives on the hill.
They dined upon mince and slices of quince,
Which they ate with a runcible spoon,
And hand in hand on the edge of the sand
They danced by the light of the moon, – the moon,
They danced by the light of the moon.

🐾 *Edward Lear* (1812–1888), poet and artist

Our mother was the Pussy-Cat, our father was the
    Owl,
And so we're partly little beasts and partly little fowl,
The brothers of our family have feathers and they
    hoot,
While all the sisters dress in fur and have long tails
    to boot.
We all believe that little mice,
For food are singularly nice.

Our mother died long years ago. She was a lovely cat,
Her tail was five feet long and grey with stripes, but
    what of that?

In Sila forest on the East of far Calabria's shore
She tumbled from a lofty tree – none ever saw her
  more.
Our owly father long was ill from sorrow and
  surprise,
But with the feathers of his tail he wiped his weeping
  eyes.
And in the hollow of a tree in Sila's inmost maze
We made a happy home and there we pass our
  obvious days.

🐾 *Edward Lear* (1812–1888), poet and artist

To see a high-bred horse when prancing,
                is no news;
  But to see a cat fiddling and mice all dancing,
                is strange indeed!
      Come foot it, my dears,
      And when you've done,
      I'll eat you for supper,
      Aye, every one.

To see wrestlers kicking shins,
>Is no news;
But to see cats playing at ninepins,
>Is strange indeed!
>I'll lay a penny,
>You don't get many.
>I'll knock down all,
>>And swallow the ball.

🐾 *Anonymous ballad*, 'The World Turned Upside Down'

My dear Agnes,

   . . . Three visitors came knocking at my door, begging me to let them in. And when I opened the door, who do you think they were? You'll never guess. Why, they were three cats! Wasn't it curious? However, they all looked so cross and disagreeable that I took up the first thing I could lay my hand on (which happened to be a rolling pin) and knocked them all down as flat as pancakes! 'If you come knocking at *my* door,' I said, '*I* shall come

knocking at *your* heads.' That was fair, wasn't it?
Yours affectionately,
Lewis Carroll

My dear Agnes,

About the cats, you know. Of course I didn't leave
them lying flat on the ground like dried flowers: no, I
picked them up, and I was as kind as I could be to
them. I lent them the portfolio for a bed – they
wouldn't have been comfortable in a real bed, you
know: they were too thin – but they were *quite* happy
between the sheets of blotting-paper – and each of
them had a pen-wiper for a pillow. Well, then I went
to bed: but first I lent them three dinner-bells, to
ring if they wanted anything in the night . . .

In the morning I gave them some rat-tail jelly and
buttered mice for breakfast and they were as discon-
tented as they could be. They wanted some boiled
pelican, but of course I knew it wouldn't be good for
them. So all I said was 'Go to Number Two,
Finborough Road, and ask for Agnes Hughes, and if
it's *really* good for you, she'll give some.' Then I shook
hands with them all, and wished them goodbye, and

drove them up the chimney. They seemed very sorry to go, and they took the bells and portfolio with them. I didn't find this out till after they had gone, and then I was sorry too, and wished for them back again . . .

🐾 *Lewis Carroll*, Letter to Agnes Hughes, 1869

Three little kittens lost their mittens,
And they began to cry:
'Oh, mother dear,
We very much fear,
That we have lost our mittens!'

'Lost your mittens,
You naughty kittens!
Then you shall have no pie.'
'Mee-ow, mee-ow, mee-ow.'
'No you shall have no pie.'
'Mee-ow, mee-ow, mee-ow!'

Three little kittens found their mittens,
And they began to cry:

'Oh, mother dear,
See here – see here!
See, we have found our mittens.'

'Put on your mittens,
You silly kittens,
And you may have some pie.'
'Purr, purr, purr,
Oh, let us taste the pie!
Purr, purr, purr.'

Three little kittens put on their mittens,
And soon ate up the pie,
'Oh mother dear,
We greatly fear,
That we have soiled our mittens.'

'Soiled your mittens,
You naughty kittens!'
Then they began to sigh:
'Mee-ow, mee-ow, mee-ow!'
Then they began to sigh:
'Mee-ow, mee-ow, mee-ow.'

Three little kittens washed their mittens
And hung them out to dry:
'Oh, mother dear,
Do you now hear,
That we have washed our mittens?'

'Washed your mittens!
Then you're good kittens:
But I smell a rat close by!'
'Hush, hush! Mee-ow, mee-ow!
We smell a rat close by!
Mee-ow mee-ow, mee-ow!'

🐾 *Anonymous*

There was an old man on the Border,
Who lived in the utmost disorder;
He danced with the cat, and made tea in his hat,
Which vexed all the folks on the Border.

🐾 *Edward Lear* (1812–1888), poet and artist

As I was going o'er misty moor
I spied three cats at a mill door.
One was white, and one was black,
And one was like my granny's cat.
I hopped o'er the style and broke my heel,
I flew to Ireland very weel,
Spied an old woman sat by the fire,
Sowing silk, jinking keys;
Cat's in the cream pot up to her knees,
Hen's in the hurdle crowing for day,
Cock's in the barn threshing corn,
I ne'er saw the like since I was born.

Anonymous, 'The Bull's in the Barn'

There was a little cat,
And she caught a little rat,
Which she dutifully rendered to her mother –
Who said 'Bake him in a pie,
For his flavour's very high,
Or confer him on the poor if you'd rather.'

🐾 **Mark Twain** *(Samuel Langhorne Clemens)*
(1835–1910), novelist

Two little kittens, one stormy night
Began to quarrel and then to fight;
One had a mouse, the other had none,
And that was the way the quarrel begun.

'I'll have that mouse!' said the bigger cat;
'You'll have that mouse? We'll see about that.'
'I will have that mouse,' said the elder one;
'You shan't have that mouse,' said the little one.

I told you before 'twas a stormy night,
When these two little kittens began to fight,

The old woman seized her sweeping broom
And swept the two kittens right out of the room.

The ground was covered with frost and snow,
And the two little kittens had nowhere to go;
So they laid them down on the mat at the door,
While the angry old woman was sweeping the floor.

And then they crept in as quiet as mice,
All wet with snow and as cold as ice,
For they found it was better, that stormy night,
To lie down and sleep than to quarrel and fight.

🐾 *Anonymous*

We're all in the dumps
For diamonds are trumps,
The kittens are gone to St Paul's,
The babies are bit,
The moon's in a fit,
And the houses are built without walls.

🐾 *Anonymous*

Hoddley, poddley, puddles and fogs,
Cats are to marry poodle dogs;
Cats in blue jackets and dogs in red hats,
What will become of the mice and the rats?

 Anonymous

Chapter Five

Miniature Tigers

But cats resemble tigers? They are tigers in miniature?
Well, – and very pretty miniatures they are.

🐾 *Leigh Hunt (1784–1859)*, poet and writer

She sights a Bird – she chuckles –
She flattens – then she crawls –
She runs without the look of feet –
Her eyes increase to Balls –

Her Jaws stir – twitching – hungry –
Her Teeth can hardly stand –
She leaps, but Robin leaped the first –
Ah, Pussy, of the Sand.

The Hopes so juicy ripening –
You almost bathed your Tongue –
When Bliss disclosed a hundred Toes –
And fled with every one –

😼 *Emily Dickinson* *(1830–1886)*, poet

When the family has finished tea, and gathers round
the fire to enjoy the hours of indigestion, the cat
slouches casually out of the room and disappears.
Life, true life, now begins for him. He saunters
down his own backyard, springs to the top of the
fence with one easy bound, drops lightly down on
the other side, trots across the right-of-way to a
vacant allotment, and skips to the roof of an empty
shed. As he goes, he throws off the effeminacy of
civilisation; his gait becomes lithe and pantherlike;
he looks quickly and keenly from side to side, and
moves noiselessly, for he has so many enemies –
dogs, cabmen with whips, and small boys with
stones. Arrived on the top of the shed, the cat
arches his back, rakes his claws once or twice

through the soft bark of the old roof, wheels round and stretches himself a few times; just to see that every muscle is in full working order; then, dropping his head nearly to his paws, he sends across a league of backyards his call to his kindred—a call to love, or war, or sport. Before long they come, gliding, graceful shadows, approaching circuitously, and halting occasionally to reconnoiter – tortoiseshell, tabby, and black, all domestic cats, but all transformed for the nonce into their natural state. No longer are they the hypocritical, meek creatures who an hour ago were cadging for fish and milk. They are now ruffling, swaggering blades with a Gascon sense of dignity. Their fights are grim and determined, and a cat will be clawed to ribbons before he will yield. Even young lady cats have this inestimable superiority over human beings, that they can work off jealousy, hatred, and malice in a sprawling, yelling combat on a flat roof. All cats fight, and all keep themselves more or less in training while they are young. Your cat may be the acknowledged lightweight champion of his district – a Griffo of the feline ring! Just think how much more he gets out

of his life than you do out of yours – what a
hurricane of fighting and lovemaking his life is –
and blush for yourself . . .

🐾 *Banjo Paterson* (1864–1941), poet and writer

The phrase 'domestic cat' is an oxymoron.

🐾 *Anonymous*

A perverse habit of cat-goddesses
Even the blackest of them, black as coals
Save for a new moon blazing on each breast,
With coral tongues and beryl eyes like lamps,
Long-leggèd, pacing three by three in nines
This obstinate habit is to yield themselves
In verisimilar love-ecstasies,
To tatter-eared and slinking alley-toms
No less below the common run of cats
Than they above it; which they do for spite,
To provoke jealousy – not the least abashed

By such gross-headed, rabbit-coloured litters
As soon they shall be happy to desert.

🐾 **Robert Graves** *(1895–1985)*,
'Cat-Goddesses'

Ignorant people think it's the noise which fighting
cats make that is so aggravating, but it ain't so; it's
the sickening grammar they use.

🐾 **Mark Twain** *(Samuel Langhorne Clemens)*
(1835–1910), novelist

A labouring man returning to his cottage after night-
fall, passed by a lone house in ruins, long uninhab-
ited. Surprised at the appearance of light within, and
strange sounds issuing from the desolate interior, he
stopped and looked in at one of the windows, and
there in a large old gloomy room, quite bare of
furniture except that cobwebs hung about its walls
like tapestry, he beheld a marvellous spectacle. A

small coffin covered with a pall stood in the midst of the floor, and round and round about it, with dismal lamentations in the feline tongue, marched a circle of cats, one of them being covered from head to foot with a black veil, and walking as chief mourner. The man was so frightened with what he saw that he waited to see no more, but went straight home, and at supper told his wife what had befallen him. Their own old cat, who had been sitting as was her wont, on the elbow of her master's chair, kept her station very quietly, till he came to the description of the chief mourner, when, to the great surprise of the old couple, she bounced up and flew up the chimney exclaiming – 'Then I am King of the Cats.'

🐾 **Robert Southey** *(1774–1843)*, poet

Once cats were all wild, but afterward they retired to houses, wherefore there are plenty of them in all countries.

🐾 **Edward Topsell**, 'The History of Four-Footed Beasts', 1607

The cats as other creatures do,
Used to swagger and make love too.
And in the dark and coldest night
These Jeffry Lyons use to fight:
Then they cry 'Mew, puss, mew.'
But the cruel'st battle far,
Was lately fought at Temple Bar
Upon the tiles o' the houses there;
Where Bowlo Sir Bore cat was heard to swear
'The slave that courts my puss shall die.'
To whom Sir Sharp Nail gives the lie.
Then they cry, 'Mew, puss, mew,'
And so they fiercely both sides join,
Asking 'Who shall tear thy coat and mine?'
    'Thou and I,'
Then they cry, 'Mew,'
Still they cry, 'Mew.'

🐾 **William Lawes** *(1602–1645),* 'The Cats'

As the lion is a solitary animal, so the cat is a moon-struck beast. Its eyes, clear-visioned and glittering in the darkest nights, wax and wane in imitation of the moon; for as the moon, according as she shares in the light of the sun, changes her face every day, so is the cat moved by a similar affection towards the moon, its pupils waxing and waning at the times when that heavenly body is crescent or in its decline. Several naturalists assert that when the moon is at its full, cats have more strength and cunning to make war upon mice than when it is weak.

🐾 *Vulson de la Clombière*, 'Livre de la Science Heroïque', 1639

Oh Auntie, isn't he a beauty! And is he a gentleman or a lady?

– Neither, my dear! I had him fixed. It saves him from so many undesirable associations.

🐾 *D. H. Lawrence* (1885–1930), 'Puss Puss'

The tom cat is extremely lustful, but the female cat is devoted to her kittens and tries to avoid sexual intercourse with the male, because the semen which he ejaculates is exceedingly hot and like fire and burns her. Now the tom cat knowing this, kills their kittens, and the female in her yearning for kittens yields to his lust. They say cats hate and abhor all foul-smelling objects, and that is why they dig a hole before they urinate or defecate, so that they hide it from their sight by throwing earth on it.

Claudius Aelian *(AD 175–235)*, 'On the Nature of Animals'

well boss
mehitabel the cat
has reappeared in her old
haunts with a
flock of kittens
three of them this time

archy she said to me
yesterday
the life of a female
artist is continually
hampered what in hell
have i done to deserve
all these kittens

i look back on my life
and it seems to me to be
just one damned kitten
after another
i am a dancer archy
and my only prayer
is to be allowed
to give my best to my art
but just as i feel
that i am succeeding
in my life work
along comes another batch
of these damned kittens
it is not archy
that i am shy on mother love
god knows i care for

the sweet little things
curse them
but am i never to be allowed
to live my own life
i have purposely avoided
matrimony in the interests
of the higher life
but i might just
as well have been a domestic
slave for all the freedom
i have gained
i hope none of them
gets run over by
an automobile
my heart would bleed
if anything happened
to them and i found it out
but it isn t fair archy
it isn t fair
these damned tom cats have all
the fun and freedom
if i was like some of these
green eyed feline vamps i know
i would simply walk out on the

bunch of them and
let them shift for themselves
but i am not that kind
archy i am full of mother love
my kindness has always
been my curse
a tender heart is the cross i bear
self sacrifice always and forever
is my motto damn them
i will make a home
for the sweet innocent
little things
unless of course providence
in his wisdom should remove
them they are living
just now in an abandoned
garbage can just behind
a made over stable in greenwich
village and if it rained
into the can before i could
get back and rescue them
i am afraid the little
dears might drown

it makes me shudder just
to think of it
of course if i were a family cat
they would probably
be drowned anyhow
sometimes i think
the kinder thing would be
for me to carry the
sweet little things
over to the river
and drop them in myself
but a mother s love archy
is so unreasonable
something always prevents me
these terrible
conflicts are always
presenting themselves
to the artist
the eternal struggle
between art and life archy
is something fierce
my what a dramatic life i have lived
one moment up the next

moment down again
but always gay archy always gay
and always the lady too
in spite of hell
well boss it will
be interesting to note
just how mehitabel
works out her present problem
a dark mystery still broods
over the manner
in which the former
family of three kittens
disappeared
one day she was talking to me
of the kittens
and the next day when i asked
her about them
she said innocently
what kittens
interrogation point
and that was all
i could ever get out
of her on the subject

we had a heavy rain
right after she spoke to me
but probably that garbage can
leaks so the kittens
have not yet
been drowned

🐾 *Archy the cockroach* (Don Marquis)
(1878–1937), 'Mehitabel and her Kittens'

Cats too, with what silent stealthiness, with what
light steps do they creep towards a bird! How slily
they will sit and watch, and then dart out upon a
mouse! These animals scratch up the earth and bury
their ordure, being well aware that the smell of it
would betray their presence.

🐾 *Pliny the Elder*, 'The Natural History', AD 77

December 12, 1856. Wonderful, wonderful is our life, and that of our companions! That there should be such a thing as a brute animal, not human! that it should attain to a sort of our society with our race! Think of cats, for instance; they are neither Chinese nor Tartars, they neither go to school, nor read the Testament. Yet how near they come to doing so, how much they are like us who do.

October 29, 1858. The cat comes stealthily creeping towards some prey amid the withered flowers in the garden, which being disturbed by my approach, she runs low toward it, with an unusual glare or superficial light in her eye, ignoring her oldest acquaintance, as wild as her remotest ancestor . . .

September 28, 1859. As the lion is said to lie in a thicket or in tall reeds and grass by day, slumbering, and sally out at night, just so with the cat. She will ensconce herself for the day in the grass or weeds in some out-of-the-way nook near the house, and arouse herself toward night.

🐾 *Henry David Thoreau* *(1817–1862)*,
philosopher

Every branch big with it,
Bent every twig with it;
Every fork like a white web-foot;
Every street and pavement mute:
Some flakes have lost their way, and grope back
    upward, when
Meeting those meandering down they turn and
    descend again.
The palings are glued together like a wall,
And there is no waft of wind with the fleecy fall.

A sparrow enters the tree,
Whereon immediately
A snow-lump thrice his own slight size
Descends on him and showers his head and eyes.
And overturns him,

And near inurns him,
And lights on a nether twig, when its brush
Starts off a volley of other lodging lumps with a rush.

The steps are a blanched slope,
Up which, with feeble hope,
A black cat comes, wide-eyed and thin:
And we take him in.

🐾 *Thomas Hardy*, 'Snow in the Suburbs', 1925

Disassociate the luxury-loving cat from the atmosphere
of social comfort in which it usually contrives to
move, and observe it critically under the adverse
conditions of civilization – that civilisation which can
impel a man to the degradation of clothing himself in
tawdry ribald garments and capering mountebank
dances in the streets for the earning of the few coins
that keep him on the respectable, or non-criminal,
side of society. The cat of the slums and alleys,
starved, outcast, harried, still keeps amid the prowlings of its adversity the bold, free, panther-tread with

which it paced of yore the temple courts of Thebes, still displays the self-reliant watchfulness which man has never taught it to lay aside. And when its shifts and clever managings have not sufficed to stave off inexorable fate, when its enemies have proved too strong or too many for its defensive powers, it dies fighting to the last, quivering with the choking rage or mastered resistance, and voicing in its death-yell that agony of bitter remonstrance which human animals, too, have flung at the powers that may be; the last protest against a destiny that might have made them happy – and has not.

🐾 **'Saki'** Hector Hugh Munro *(1870–1913)*, writer

The Cat . . . will kill mice and he will be kind to Babies when he is in the house, just as long as they do not pull his tail too hard. But when he has done that, and between times, and when the moon gets up and night comes, he is the Cat that walks by himself, and all places are alike to him. Then he goes out to the Wet Wild Wood or up the Wet Wild Trees or on the Wet Wild Roofs, waving his tail and walking by his wild lone.

🐾 **Rudyard Kipling** *(1865–1936)*, 'The Cat that Walked by Himself'

The cat went here and there
And the moon spun round like a top,
And the nearest kin of the moon,
The creeping cat, looked up.
Black Minnaloushe stared at the moon,
For, wander and wail as he would,
The pure cold light in the sky
Troubled his animal blood.
Minnaloushe runs in the grass
Lifting his delicate feet.
Do you dance, Minnaloushe, do you dance?
When two close kindred meet,
What better than call a dance?
Maybe the moon may learn,
Tired of that courtly fashion,

A new dance turn.
Minnaloushe creeps through the grass
From moonlit place to place,
The sacred moon overhead
Has taken a new phase.
Does Minnaloushe know that his pupils
Will pass from change to change,
And that from round to crescent,
From crescent to round they range?
Minnaloushe creeps through the grass
Alone, important and wise,
And lifts to the changing moon
His changing eyes.

🐾 *William Butler Yeats* (1865–1939), 'The
  Cat and the Moon'

Cats are of divers colours but for the most part
griseld, like to congealed ice, which cometh from
the condition of her meat: her head is like unto the
head of a lion, except in her sharp ears; her flesh is

soft and smooth; her eyes glister above measure, especially when a man cometh to see them on the suddain, and in the night they can hardly be endured, for their flaming aspect. Wherefore Democritus describing the Persian Smaragde saith that is it not transparent, but filleth the eye with pleasant brightness, such as is in the eyes of panthers and cats, for they cast forth beams in the shadow and darkness, but in sunshine they have no such clearness . . . Albertus compareth their eyesight to carbuncles in dark places, because in the night they can see perfectly to kill rats and mice: the root of the herb Valerian.. is very like to the eye of a cat, and wheresoever it groweth, if cats come thereunto, they instantly dig it up, for love thereof, as I myself have seen in mine own garden, and not once only, but often, even then when as I had caused it to be hedged or compassed round about with thorns, for it smelleth marvellous like to a cat. The Egyptians have observed in the eyes of a cat, the increase of the moonlight, . . . and the male cat doth also vary his eyes with the sun; for when the sun ariseth, the apple of his eye is long; toward noon it is round, and at the evening it cannot be seen at all, but the whole eye sheweth alike.

🐾 *Edward Topsell*, 'The History of Four-Footed Beasts', 1607

The crafty cat, a buff-black Siamese,
Sniffing through the wild wood, sagely, silently goes,
Prick ears, lank legs, alertly twitching nose,
And on her secret errand reads with ease
A language no man knows.

🐾 *Walter de La Mare* (1873–1956), 'Double Dutch'

May 6 1780. I opened a hen swift, which a cat had caught, and found she was in high condition, very plump & fat . . . Cats often catch swifts as they stoop to go up under the eaves of low houses.

July 15, 1786. The cat gets on the roof of the house, & catches young bats as they come forth from behind the sheet of lead at the bottom of the chimney.

March 16 1787. The cats brought in a dead house martin from the stable. I was in hopes at first sight that it might have been in a torpid state; but it was decayed and dry.

April 18 1790. A boy has taken three little young squirrels in their nest, or drey, as it is called in these parts. These small creatures he put under the care of a cat who had lately lost her kittens, & finds that she nurses & suckles them with the same assiduity & affection, as if they were her own offspring. . . . So many people went to see the little squirrels suckled by a cat, that the foster mother became jealous of her charge, & in pain for the safety; & therefore hid them over the ceiling, where one died. This circumstance shews her affection for these foundlings, & that she supposes the squirrels to be her own young.

🐾 *Gilbert White (1720–1793),* naturalist

But God it woot, there may no man embrace
As to distrain a thing which that nature
Hath naturally set in a creature . . .
Let take a cat and foster him well with milk
And tender flesh and make his couch of silk,
And let him seen a mouse go by the wall,
Anon he waveth milk and flesh and all,
And every dainty that is in that house,
Such appetite he hath to eat a mouse.

🐾 *Geoffrey Chaucer* *(1343–1400)* poet

One night an old woman was sitting up very late
spinning when a knocking came to the door. 'Who's
there?' she asked. No answer; but still the knocking
went on. 'Who is there?' she asked a second time. No
answer; and the knocking continued.

'Who is there?' she asked a third time in a very
angry passion.

Then there came a small voice – 'Ah, Judy, agrah,
let me in, for I am cold and hungry: open the door,
Judy, agrah, and let me sit by the fire, for the night is

cold out there. Judy, agrah, let me in, let me in!'

The heart of Judy was touched, for she thought it was some small child that had lost its way, and she rose up from her spinning, and went and opened the door – when in walked a large black cat with a white breast, and two white kittens after her.

They all made over to the fire and began to warm and dry themselves, purring all the time very loudly; but Judy said never a word, only went on spinning.

Then the black cat spoke at last – 'Judy, agrah, don't stay up so late again, for the fairies wanted to hold a council there tonight, and to have some supper but you have prevented them; so they were very angry and determined to kill you, and only for myself and my two daughters here you would have been dead by this time. So take my advice, don't interfere with the fairy hours again, for the night is theirs, and they hate to look on the face of a mortal when they are out for pleasure or business. So I ran on to tell you, and now give me a drink of milk, for I must be off.'

And after the milk was finished the cat stood up, and called her daughter to come away.

'Good night, Judy, agrah,' she said. 'You have been

very civil to me, and I'll not forget it to you. Good night, good night.'

With that the black cat and the two kittens whisked up the chimney; but Judy looking down saw something glittering on the hearth, and taking it up she found it was a piece of silver, more than she could ever make in a month by her spinning, and she was glad in her heart, and never again sat up so late to interfere with the fairy hours, but the black cat and her daughters came not more to the house.

Lady Speranza Wilde, 'Ancient Legends, Mystic Charms and Superstitions of Ireland', 1887

Ye cats that at midnight spit love at each other,
Who best feel the pangs of a passionate lover,
I appeal to your scratches and your tattered fur,
If the business of love be no more than to purr.
Old Lady Grimalkin with her gooseberry eyes,
Knew something when a kitten, for why she was wise;
You find by experience, the love-fit's soon o'er,
Puss! Puss! lasts not long, but turns to *Cat-whore!*

Men ride many miles,
Cats tread many tiles,
Both hazard their necks in the fray;
Only cats, when they fall
From a house or a wall,
Keep their feet, mount their tails, and away!

🐾 *Thomas Flatman* (1637–1688), 'An Appeal
to Cats in the Business of Love'

I tell you how easy it is to be 'taken in'. Fix on your
house, and mew piteously at the back door. When
it is opened, run in and rub yourself against the
first leg you come across. Rub hard, and look up
confidingly. Nothing gets round human beings, I
have noticed, quicker than confidence. They don't
get much of it, and it pleases them. Always be
confiding. At the same time, be prepared for
emergencies. If you are still doubtful as to your
reception, try and get yourself slightly wet. Why
people should prefer a wet cat to a dry one I have
never been able to understand, but that a wet cat is

practically sure of being taken in and gushed over, while a dry cat is liable to have the garden hose turned upon it, is an undoubted fact. Also, if you can possibly manage it, and if it is offered to you, eat a bit of dried bread. The Human Race is always stirred to its deepest depths by the sight of a cat eating a bit of dry bread.

Jerome K Jerome (1859–1927), author and humourist

A downy cove is our old tom cat,
Just turned thirty years old;
He eateth the lean, and leaveth the fat,
And won't touch his meals when too cold.
His food must be crumbled, and not decayed,
To pleasure his dainty whim,
But a turkey bone from the kitchen-maid
Is a very good meal for him.
Chorus: Creeping over the tiles pit pat,
                    A downy cove is the old tom cat.

Whole joints have fled, and their bones decayed,
And dishes have broken been,
But old tom still follows the kitchen-maid,
And slyly licks up the cream.
Now, old tom cat, in his lonely days,
Shall joyously think of the past,
And a big leg of mutton, that never was touched,
Shall be food for our Tommy at last.

Fast creepeth he, though he hath no wings,
And a sly old dodger is he,
As under the garret window he sings –
Ain't you coming out tonight, love, to me?
Then slyly he creepeth the gutters all round,
And his old tail he joyously waves,
As his lady love from a garret he spies,
And he sings his amorous staves.

🐾 *Anonymous*, Music Hall song, c. 1855

This beast is called a 'Masion' (cat) for that he is enemy to mice and rats. He is sly and witty, and seeth so sharply that he overcometh darkness of the night by the shining light of his eyne. In shape of body he is like unto a leopard, and hath a great mouth. He doth delight that he enjoyeth his liberty; and in his youth he is swift, pliant and merry. He maketh a ruthful noise and a gastful when he profereth to fight with another. He is a cruel beast when he is wild, and falleth on his own feet from, most high places: and is never hurt therewith. When he hath a fair skin, he is, as it were, proud thereof, and then he goeth much about to be seen.

🐾 *John Bossewell*, 'Workes of Armorie', 1597

There once was a Grand Duke of Baden
Said 'The things that go on in my garden!
I really can't stand;
Not a cat in the land
But gives itself heirs in my garden.'

🐾 *'Saki'* Hector Hugh Munro (1870–1916), writer

I am sorry to say that the cats are more mischievous than ever. They got into the greenhouse last night – broke one of our best geraniums to pieces – tore a good deal of a night-scented stock – dragged my sofa-cover all over the floor, and danced all over the looking glass. They have also scratched up our new border of red and blue flowers under the jessamine, and are really past bearing – particularly the white one, for I don't think the tabby would be so bad if alone.

🐾 *Mary Russell Mitford*, Letter, 1834

Midnight's bell goes ring, 'ting, ting, ting, ting';
The dogs do howl, and not a bird does sing
But the nightingale, and she cries 'twit, twit, twit,
    twit';
Owls then on every bough do sit;
Ravens croak on chimney tops;
The cricket in the chamber hops;
And the cats cry 'mew, mew, mew';
The nibbling mouse is not asleep,

But he goes 'peep, peep, peep, peep, peep';
And the cats cry 'mew, mew, mew';
And still the cats cry 'mew, mew, mew'.

🐾 *Thomas Middleton* (1580–1627), playwright

Why should a black cat be thought so widely different
from all others by the foolish, unthinking, and ignorant?
Why simply on account of its colour being black should
it have ascribed to it a numberless variety of bad omens,
besides having certain necromantic power? In Germany,
for instance, black cats are kept away from children as
omens of evil, and if a black cat appeared in the room
of one lying ill it was said to portend death. To meet a
black cat in the twilight was held unlucky. In 'the good
old days' a black cat was generally the only colour that
was favoured by men reported to be wizards and also
were said to be the constant companions of reputed
witches, and in such a horror and detestation were they
then held that when the unfortunate creatures were ill-
treated, drowned or even burned, very frequently we are
told that their cats suffered martyrdom at the same

time . . . For some reason or other, the black cat is held by the prejudiced ignorant as an animal most foul and detestable, and wonderful stories are related of their actions in the dead of night during thunder storms and windy nights. Yet, as far as I can discover, there appears little difference either of temper or habit in the black cat distinct from that of any other colour, though it is maintained by many even to this day that black cats are far more vicious and spiteful and of higher courage, and this last I admit.

🐾 *Harrison Weir*, 'Our Cats', 1889

Your friskings, crawlings, squalls, I much approve:
Your spittings, pawings, high-raised rumps,
Swelled tails, and merry-andrew jumps,
With the wild minstrelsy of rapturous love.
How sweetly roll your gooseberry eyes,
As loud you tune our amorous cries,
And, loving, scratch each other black and blue.

🐾 *Peter Pindar (John Wolcot) (1738–1819)*, 'An Ode to Eight Cats'

It had been discovered that for twenty five years past an oral addition to the written standing orders of the native guard at Government House, near Poona, had been communicated regularly from one guard to another, on relief, to the effect that any cat passing out of the front door after dark was to be regarded as His Excellency the Governor, and to be saluted accordingly. The meaning of this was that Sir Robert Grant, Governor of Bombay, had died there in 1838, and on the evening of the day of his death, a cat was seen to leave the house by the front door and walk up and down a particular path, as had been the Governor's habit to do, after sunset. A Hindu sentry had observed this and he mentioned it to others of his faith, who made it a subject of superstitious conjecture, the result being that one of the priestly class had explained the mystery of the dogma of the transmigration of soul from one body to another, and interpreted the circumstances to mean that the spirit of the deceased Governor had entered into one of the House pets. It was difficult to fix on a particular one, and it was therefore decided that every cat passing out of the main entrance after dark was to be regarded as the tabernacle of Governor Grant's soul, and to be treated with due respect and the proper honours. This decision was accepted without question by all the native attendants and others belonging to Government House. The whole guard from sepoy to subahdar fully acquiesced in it, and an oral addition was made to the standing orders that the sentry at the front door would 'present arms' to any cat passing out there after dark.

🐾 **Sir Thomas Gordon**, 'A Varied Life', 1906

Chapter Six

Mad About Cats

Sir Winston Churchill adored cats and found their company soothing. Two lived with him at No 10 Downing Street. They were black mogs and were often paid more attention than assorted Field Marshals and Cabinet Ministers. The first, simply called Cat, ran off after Churchill shouted at it. The old man was deeply upset at this and ordered his secretary to put a notice in the window which said, 'Cat, come home, all is forgiven.' The cat duly returned and Churchill ordered it be plied with luxury food. Remember, this was wartime when rationing was at its height. The second black cat was called Nelson (after Churchill's favourite hero) and stayed with him all through World War Two. It was he who would sit on the Cabinet Room table alongside Winston during vital meetings about the progress (or lack of it) of the war. Sometimes, Churchill, pondering the answer to a complex problem, would turn to the cat and ask: 'Mr Cat – what is your answer to the situation confronting us?' Sir Jock Colville, his private secretary, told me this years ago during an interview. He also gave the old man a marmalade cat, called Jock, which adored Winston and was actually on his bed when he died in 1965. The cat lived out his days at Chartwell and there have been two marmalade cats – Jock II and Jock III – at the house since. (Jock III is known as 'Lord Warden of the Cinque Mouseholes'.) Churchill would often work with a cat draped around his neck like a scarf as he worked on his papers in bed. His pet budgie would often perch on his head, too.

🐾 *Paul Callan*, Letter, 2007.

We chose a fine tortoiseshell as our drawing room cat, and directly we had pronounced our decision in his favour he jumped on our shoulders and rubbed himself against our cheeks. Then with a look of regret the other cats went away . . . Christmas is

drawing on, and my sister's heart and mine are over-
flowing with love and kindness, especially towards
cats, and we cannot forget the sadness with which the
rejected pussies went away when our choice fell on
the tortoiseshell. So my dear sister and I have taken
counsel together. We must make amends to these
poor cats whom we rejected. We cannot bear to hurt
the feelings of anyone – especially a cat – and so
Jemima and I have been thinking how we could make
up to the dear creatures for their disappointment, and
we have resolved to give them a Christmas Tree. We
have informed the tortoiseshell of our resolution, and
he approves. We have not seen him much since,
except at meal times, when of course he is present. At
other times we suspect he is rambling round among
his friends and acquaintances informing them of our
intention, and inviting them to our Christmas Tree.

We have got a beautiful spruce fir, and it is
covered with candles. Also that sardine tin which was
opened when poor Agag died having been found to
be mouldy, the mouldy sardines have been taken out
and wiped, and are hung to the branches of the tree.
My sister and I think that no presents we could make

– except, perhaps, live robins – could prove more attractive to the cats. My sister and I both strongly object to cats taking live birds, and we are thankful to say that the tortoiseshell has taken the pledge and the red ribbon, which ensures his total abstinence from live robins, or bullfinch, or sparrows, or tom-tits, or cormorants, or albatrosses, or any other volatile creature. My sister and I have also assumed the red ribbon, not that we are addicted to live birds but for the sake of example to our cats.

You have no idea how pretty our Christmas Tree looks with its candles, heavy with sprats and sardines. Tonight, at six o'clock, the candles will be lighted, and the doors flung open, and – Come and see! Come, and see the cats enjoy their Christmas Tree.

🐾 *Rev. Sabine Baring Gould*, 'The Prague Pig', 1890

Sir – My late mother-in-law always hung her Christmas tree upside down. Each December she unwrapped the artificial tree, suspended it by its base from a beam and then decorated it. She did this as a preventive measure against cats attacking the festive baubles. People thought she was daft because she didn't have any cats. But the cats were ours – Octopussy and Scoon, visitors to her home at Christmas.

David Chapman, Letter, November 2007

St Jerome in his study kept a great big cat,
It's always in his pictures, with its feet upon the mat.
Did he give it milk to drink, in a little dish?
When it came to Fridays, did he give it fish?
If I lost my little cat, I should be sad without it.
I should ask St Jerome what to do about it.
I should ask St Jerome, just because of that
He's the only saint I know that kept a pussy cat.

Anonymous

Mrs Dilke has two cats – a mother and a daughter –
now the mother is a tabby and the daughter a black
and white like the spotted child – Now it appears
ominous to me for the doors of both houses are
opened frequently, so that there is a complete
thoroughfare for both cats (there being no board up
to the contrary) they may one and several of them
come into my room at libitum. But no – the tabby
only comes – whether from sympathy from Anne the
maid or me I cannot tell – or whether Brown (a
friend) has left behind him any atmospheric spirit of
maidenhood I cannot tell. The cat is not an old maid
herself – her daughter is proof of it – I have ques-
tioned her – I have looked at the lines of her paw – I
have felt her pulse – to no purpose. Why should the
old cat come to me? I ask myself – and my self has
not a word to answer.

 **John Keats**, letter to his brother, January,
1819

Cat! who hast pass'd thy grand climateric,
How many mice and rats hast in thy days
Destroyed? How many titbits stolen? Gaze
With those bright languid segments green and prick
Those velvet ears – but prythee do not stick
Thy latent talons in me – and upraise
Thy gentle mew – and tell me all thy frays
Of fish and mice, and rats and tender chick.
Nay look not down, nor lick thy dainty wrists –
For all the wheezy asthma – and for all
The tail's tip is nicked off – and though the fists
Of many a maid have given thee many a maul,
Still is that fur as soft as when the lists
In youth thou enter'dst on glass bottled wall.

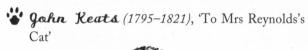 **John Keats** *(1795–1821)*, 'To Mrs Reynolds's
Cat'

Jacobus Diaconus, in the *Life of St Gregory the Great*, who died AD 604, speaking of that mild and benevolent pontiff, after he had retired from all secular employments to live in a monastery, says, 'He possessed nothing in the world except a cat, which he carried in his bosom, frequently caressing it, as his sole companion.'

🐾 *Rev. Samuel Lysons*, 'The Model Merchant of the Middle Ages', 1860

The great manager (John Rich, theatre manager of Covent Garden) was lolling in ungraceful ease on a sofa, holding a play in one hand, and in the other a teacup, from which he sipped frequently. Around him were seven and twenty cats of all sizes, colours and kinds. Toms and tabbies, old cats and kittens, tortoise-shells, Maltese, brindles, white, black and yellow cats of every description. Some were frisking over the floor, others asleep on the rug; one was licking the buttered toast on his breakfast plate, another was engaged in drinking the cream for his tea, two cats lay on his knee, one was asleep on his shoulder, and another sat demurely on his head. Peg Woffington was astounded at the sight. Rich to her mind had for many years been the greatest man in the world. The menagerie of grimalkins, amid which he lay so carelessly, was so different an environment from her conception of the study of the Convent Garden theatre manager, that she was embarrassed into silence.

🐾 *Augustin Daly*, 'Woffington: a Tribute to the Actress and the Woman', 1888

Dearest cat, honoured guest of my old house,
Arch your supple, tingling back,
And curl upon my knee, to let me
Bathe my fingers in your warm fur.

Green eyes half-closed mock me as they caress,
After a slow, luxurious shudder.
Gold-flecked and drowsy, your eyes
Watch me, ironic yet benign.

Not for you, my philosophic old friend,
The blind devotion of a boisterous dog,
Yet my heart tells me that you love me still.

Your fleeting though understanding love
Satisfies me; and in you, serene thinker, I hail
Two subtler qualities – sweetness and doubt.

🐾 *François Lemaître* (1853–1914), dramatist
    and poet

Cats. William Laud, Archbishop of Canterbury was a
great lover of cats; he was presented with some
Cyprus cats, ie our tabby cats, which were sold at first
for £5 a piece; this was about 1637 or 1638. I do well
remember that the common English cat was white
with some bluish piedness; *silicet* a gallipot blue; the
race or breed of them are now almost lost.

🐾 *John Aubrey* (1626–1697), antiquarian

It was the maestro, Alessandro Scarlatti. A harp was leaning upon his chair in front of which, with an indescribably earnest mien and inimitable dignity, was a large black cat. He was occupying himself with flourishing the tip of his tail, which, as well as his left ear, was of a dazzling whiteness, gently over the chords, which singular experiment, very naturally, brought for all manner of strange sounds. It was his habit, in fact, since his lord and master never took his musical studies amiss, to abandon himself, every morning, with utter recklessness, to his genius, accompanying the movement of his tail with the most absurd gesture; and sometimes in the overflow of his feelings, he sang one of those ancient melancholy strains of his forefathers, which, as has been asserted, have the power to soften the hardest stone, and drive the calmest of men to madness. All this caused not the least disturbance to Master Scarlatti; on the contrary, he laughed like a good-natured devil, when-ever the cat fell into his musical ecstasies. In the evening however the cat always sat in the corner of his beloved master's room, with an expression like that of a sentimental privy counselor, and then it was the Master who played the harp. . . . What wonder if these magic tones caused the sensitive soul of the cat, who was still mourning, withal, for the death of a beloved bride, to melt, and his green eyes to overflow, like the King of Thule's! Whenever Scarlatti perceived this, he took up his faithful four-legged companion, into his lap, and stroked, caressed, and kissed him, until he had recovered his mad romping humor. On the whole, the cat led a perfectly charming life with his gentle master, to him he was all in all – friend, wife, and child, whom he never left by day or by night. When the old Master was engaged in composing something, Ponto sat quietly upon his left shoulder, and brushed his forehead softly with his famous white-tipped tail.

🐾 *Putnam's Magazine*, 'The Cat's Fugue', 1853

Stately, kindly, lordly friend,
   Condescend
Here to sit by me, and turn
Glorious eyes that smile and burn,
Golden eyes, love's lustrous meed,
On the golden page I read.

All your wondrous wealth of hair
   Dark and fair,
Silken-shaggy, soft and bright
As the clouds and beams of night,
Pays my reverent hand's caress
Back with friendlier gentleness.

Dogs may fawn on all and some
   As they come;
You, a friend of loftier mind,
Answer friends alone in kind.
Just your foot upon my hand
Softly bids it understand.

May you not rejoice as I,
   Seeing the sky

Change to heaven revealed and bid
Earth reveal the heaven it hid
All night long from stars and moon
Now the sun sets all in tune?

What within you wakes with day
      Who can say?
All too little may we tell,
Friends who like each other well,
What might haply, if we might,
Bid us read our lives aright.

Wild on woodland ways your sires
      Flashed like fires:
Fair as flame and fierce and fleet
As with wings on wingless feet
Shone and sprang your mother, free,
Bright and brave as wind or sea.

Free and proud and glad as they,
      Here today
Rests or roams their radiant child,
Vanquished not, but reconciled,

Free from curb of aught above
Save the lovely curb of love.

:•: *Algernon Swinburne* *(1837–1909)*, 'To a Cat'

I never shall forget the indulgence with which he (Samuel Johnson, the writer) treated Hodge, his cat, for whom he himself used to go out and buy oysters lest the servants, having that trouble, should take a dislike to the poor creature . . . I am unluckily one of those who have an antipathy to a cat, so that I am uneasy when in the room with one; and, I own, I frequently suffered a good deal from the presence of this same Hodge. I recollect him one day scrambling up Dr Johnson's breast, apparently with much satisfaction, while my friend, smiling and half whistling, rubbed down his back and pulled him by the tail; and when I observed he was a fine cat, saying, 'why, yes, Sir, but I have had cats whom I liked better than this;' and then, as if perceiving Hodge to be out of countenance, adding 'but he is a very fine cat, a very fine cat indeed.'

This reminds me of the ludicrous account which he gave Mr. Langton, of the despicable state of a young gentleman of good family. 'Sir, when I heart of him last, he was running about the town, shooting cats.' And then, in a sort of kindly reverie, he bethought himself of his own favourite cat, and said, 'But Hodge shan't be shot: no, no, Hodge shall not be shot.'

🐾 *James Boswell*, 'Life of Johnson', 1791

Last winter I had a visit of a week or two from my youngest niece, of nine years old. Wishing to have some small jollification before she went home, I thought it would be nice to have a pussies' tea party. After some consultation, we decided that the basis of it should be fish, so we went for some fresh herrings, and they were boiled and held in readiness. The invited guests were four grown pussies and two kittens, so we got ready four large and two small saucers; an equal strip of cold rice pudding met it transversely, forming a cross-shaped figure that left four spaces in the angles. Thick cream was poured into these spaces, and the solid portion was decorated with tiny balls of butter, one rather larger in the middle, and two smaller on each of the rays. A reserve of fish and cream was to be at hand to replenish the portions most quickly exhausted.

In the middle of the sitting room we placed a small, rather low, round table; and four stools were ranged round for the bigger pussies . . . They were to sit on the stools with their fore-paws on the edge of the tablecloth. We decided not to have flowers, because it would have overcrowded the space, as the two kittens were to be allowed to sit on the table.

At last the hour came, and meanwhile the excitement had grown intense. Five grown-ups were present, all as keenly interested as the little girl. The pussies were brought and placed on their stools, and the kittens, Chloe and Brindle, were put up to their saucers on the table. To our great delight they all took in the situation at once; there was only a little hesitation on Maggie's part; she thought it was not manners to put her paws on the tablecloth; but this was soon overcome, and they all set to work as if they were quite accustomed to tea parties and knew that nice behaviour was expected.

It was good to watch the pleasure of my little niece . . . Meanwhile the small guests were steadily eating away at their portions. Pinkieboy, as became the oldest and heaviest, finished his first, and after licking his saucer quite clean, and then his own lips, he looked round and clearly said, 'That was very good, and please I should like a little more, especially fish and cream.'

When they had all done there was a grand purring and washing of paws and faces before they got off their stools, and as they dispersed to find cosy sleeping places, as wise pussies do after a comfortable meal, we all thought that our little party had been brilliantly successful.

🐾 *Gertrude Jekyll*, 'Home and Garden', 1900

216

Poor Bob! How have I smiled to see
Thee sitting on thy master's knee?
While, pleased to stroke thy tabby coat,
Sweet purrings warbling in thy throat,
He would with rapturous hug declare,
No voice more sweet, or maid more fair . . .
Miss Betty's bedfellow, and pet,
(Too young to have another yet),
At dinner he'd beside her sit,
Fed from her mouth with sweetest bit.

🐾 *John Winstanley (1678–1751)*, 'Upon a
    Friend's Pet Cat being Sick'

In his love of birds and beasts Hawker, (the Rev.
Stephen Hawker) was like St Francis of Asissi . . .
He always kept a number of dogs and cats, which
occasionally accompanied him to church. 'In Mr
Hawker's judgement,' says a writer in the *Standard*,
'all the creatures had a certain right of admission to
God's house. He sometimes appeared at his lectern
attended by four or five cats, unusual but graceful

acolytes, who, as he assured us, allowing for an occasional display of youthful vivacity, rarely conducted themselves otherwise than with great propriety.'

At one time he had nine cats. 'In the evening,' writes a friend, 'he led them to the cat-house. They had all names. Each waited till he pronounced its name, and then jumped up to the shelf on which they reposed.' His dog, Dustyfoot, also went to church, and, like the dog in 'Woodstock', generally behaved very well there. But once, when Mr Hawker went into the pulpit, it followed him up the steps, and remained by his side to the end of the discourse. A clergyman, to whom he showed the church, writes 'I wanted to shut out my dog, but he insisted on his coming in, as much more fit than many Christians.' One of his cats he called his most righteous cat, because whenever he missed it, he generally found it waiting at the church door. A former servant at the vicarage says: 'There's no mistake about they cats. I know, cos I had to tend 'em; and some times I wished 'em further, I can tell 'e.'

C. E. Byles, 'The Life and Letters of R. S. Hawker', 1906

A surge of harmony fills limitless space;
Waves of the ether palpitate in cadence;
The imperceptible atom dances,
To a scientific rhythm, adapted to its form.

From its first glow and its first air born moment
The star rolls tracing its orbit, then retracing it,
In harmony the world vibrates under an immense arc,
And sings a deep toned hymn to its beauty.

O my happy cats! Your peaceful purring brings to us
The voice of this choir invisible that sings
The secrets of the mysterious universe.

Such low and ancient chanting! Such distinctive music!
I hear; I understand; my soul fills with poetry,
And my whole heart throbs in my verses.

🐾 *Hippolyte Taine* *(1828–1893)*, 'L'Absolu'

It was known that the Cardinal was mad about cats. In the morning, when he was getting up or when he was ill in bed, he would always have a dozen around him or on his bed, gambolling or fighting each other with sheathed claws. Two people were in charge of the cattery: they lived, not in the palace itself, but in the grounds . . . They were the ones that came in the morning and evening to feed the cardinal's cats.

Each of these quadrupeds had its own particular name. This was the state of the cat group at the death of the cardinal, and the notes relating to the character of each tom, cat or kitten. This document, which was preserved in a collection of autographs, was signed with the name of Robin Hood, the poet and jester of the cardinal.

At the time of the Richelieu's death, 14 cats were in residence, notably: Mounard le Fougueux; Mimi-Paillon; Felimare; Lucifer; Ruby the claw; Racan; Perruque; Pyramid and Thisbe. At his death the cardinal left pensions to all his cats; to some of them 20 livres; to others, 10 livres . . . (The notes had this to say about) Racan and Perruque; little cats that were born in a wig belonging to Racan, the mapmaker, academician and the most absent-minded man in France.

Racan had a female cat that he was very fond of. One day she gave birth in his wig. Despite the two kittens nesting in it, he placed it on his head anyway and went to visit the cardinal, who had asked him in order to consult him about a scene in his tragedies. At last when he was in the presence of Richelieu, he was tormented by the wriggling and clawing of the two kittens.

'What have you there, Racan?' said Richelieu, 'Is your head being eaten alive with itching?'

Racan, as well as many other little ridiculous habits, had a speech defect and could not pronounce his Rs or Cs. With a horrible grimace Racan replied to the cardinal: 'Monseigneur, after a quawter of houw, I have lumps in my head.'

'That is not surprising,' replied the cardinal, laughing maliciously and surreptitiously. 'You have put on your perruque very badly – that is if you are wearing one.'

'My pewwuque is wong. It is wongly placed? It is twue, nothing more twue,' said he, seeking to placate his boss.

As he tried to rearrange his headgear properly, the two kittens fell at the feet of the cardinal making little cries.

Richelieu, in the presence of such a distraction, could not, as he usually did, stop himself bursting out aloud with laughter and, as Racan would not take back the kittens, he kept them and gave one the name of Raca, the other was called Perruque in memory of this adventure.

:pawprint: *Timothee Thim* (Leo Lespès), 'Le Petit Journal', 1864.

When staying at Cannes at Christmas 1882, I was invited by Mr Lear to go over to San Remo to spend a few days with him. Mr Lear's villa was large, and the second he had built: the first became unbearable to him from a large hotel having been planted in front of it. So he put his new house in a place by the sea, where, as he said, nothing could interrupt his light unless the fishes built. The second house was exactly like the first. This, Mr Lear explained to me, was necessary, or else Foss, his cat, might not have approved of the new villa. At breakfast the morning after I arrived, this much-thought-of, though semi-tailed, cat jumped in at the window and ate a piece of toast from my hand. This, I found, was considered an event; when visitors stayed at Villa Tennyson, Foss generally hid himself in the back regions; but his recognition of me was a sort of 'guinea stamp', which seemed to please Mr Lear greatly, and assure him of my fitness to receive the constant acts of kindness he was showing me . . . My visit to Villa Tennyson coming to an end, on the last evening after dinner he took from a place in his bureau a number of carefully cut-out backs of old envelopes, and on these he drew, to send to my sister, then eight years old, the delightful series of heraldic pictures of his cat. After he had done seven he said it was a great shame to caricature Foss, and laid aside the pen.

🐾 **Sir Edward Strachey**, 'Introduction to Nonsense Songs', 1894

Dr Barker kept a seraglio and colony of cats, it happened, that at the coronation of George I the Chair of State fell to his share of the spoil (as prebendary of Westminster) which he sold to some foreigner; when they packed it up, one of his favourite cats was enclosed along with it; but the Doctor pursued his treasure in a boat to Gravesend and recovered her safe. When the Doctor was disgusted with the Ministry, he gave his female cats, the names of the chief ladies about the court; and the male ones, those of the men in power, adorning them with the blue, red or green insignia of ribbons, which the persons they represented, wore.

🐾 *Rev. W. B. Daniel*, 'Rural Sports', 1813

Henry Hastings (1551–1650) was peradventure an original in our age, or rather the copy of our nobility in ancient days . . . In his house was found beef pudding and small beer in great plenty, a house not so neatly kept as to shame him or his dirty shoes, the great hall strewed with marrow bones, full of hawks' perches, hounds, spaniels, and terriers, the upper sides of the hall hung with fox skins of this and the last year's skinning, here and there a polecat intermixed, guns and keepers' and huntsmen's poles in abundance. The parlour was a large long room, as properly furnished; on a great hearth paved with brick lay some terriers and the choicest hounds and spaniels; seldom but two of the great chairs had litters of young cats in them, which were not to be disturbed, he having always three or four attending him at dinner, and a little white round stick of fourteen inches long lying by his trencher, that he might defend such meat as he had no mind to part with to them.

🐾 *Earl of Shaftesbury* *(1621–1683)*,
'Fragment of Autobiography'

Among the other important and privileged members of the household (of Sir Walter Scott) who figured in attendance at dinner was a large grey cat, who, I observed, was regaled from time to time with tit-bits from the table. This sage grimalkin was a favourite of both master and mistress, and slept at night in their room, and Scott laughingly observed, that one of the least wise parts of their establishment was, that the window was left open at night for puss to go in and out. The cat assumed a kind of ascendancy among the quadrupeds – sitting in state in Scott's armchair, and occasionally stationing himself on a chair beside the door, as if to review his subjects as they passed, giving each dog a cuff beside the ears as he went by. This clapper-clawing was always taken in good part; it appeared to be, in fact, a mere act of sovereignty on the part of grimalkin to remind the others of their vassalage; which they acknowledged by the most perfect acquiescence. A general harmony prevailed between sovereign and subjects, and they would all sleep together in the sunshine.

🐾 *Washington Irving*, 'Abbotsford and Newstead Abbey', 1850

I have (and long shall have) a white great nimble cat,
A king upon a mouse, a strong foe to the rat.
Fine ears, long tail he hath, with lion's curbed claw,
Which oft he lifteth up, and stayes his lifted paw,
Deep musing to himself, which after-mewing shows,
Till with licked beard, his eye of fire espy his foes.

Sir Philip Sidney *(1554–1568)*, courtier and
poet

The first day we had the honour of dining at the
palace of the Archbishop of Toronto, at Naples, he
said to me, 'You must pardon my passion for cats,
but I never exclude them from my dining room, and
you will find that they make excellent company.'
Between the first and second course, the door
opened, and several enormously large and beautiful
Angora cats were introduced by the names of
Pantalone, Desdemona, Othello etc.: they took their
places on chairs near the table, and were as silent, as
quiet, as motionless, and as well behaved as the most
bon ton table in London could require. On the

bishop requesting one of the chaplains to help the Signora Desdemona, the butler stepped up to his lordship, and observed, 'My lord, La Signora Desdemona will prefer waiting for the roasts.'

🐾 *Lady Morgan*, 'The Book of the Boudoir', 1829.

For I am possessed of a cat, surpassing in beauty,
From whom I take occasion to bless Almighty God.

🐾 *Christopher Smart* *(1722–1771)*, 'Jubilate Agno'

Nellie, methinks, 'twixt thee and me,
There is a kind of sympathy;
And could we interchange our nature, –
If I were cat, thou human creature, –
I should, like thee, be no great mouser,
And thou, like me, no great composer;
For, like thy plaintive mews, my muse,

With villainous whine doth fate abuse,
Because it hath not made me sleek
As golden down on Cupid's cheek;
And yet thou canst upon the rug lie
Stretch out like snail, or curled up snugly,
As if thou wert not lean and ugly;
And I, who in poetic flights
Sometimes complain of sleepless nights,
Regardless of the sun in heaven,
Am apt to doze till past eleven, –
The world would just the same go round
If I were hanged and thou wert drowned;
There is one difference, 'tis true, –
Thou dost not know it, and I do.

🐾 **Hartley Coleridge** *(1796–1849),* 'To a Cat'

(Jeremy) Bentham (the utilitarian philosopher and
social reformer) was very fond of animals, particularly
'pussies', as he called them, when they had domestic
virtues, but he had no particular affection for the
common race of cats. He had one, however, of

which he used to boast that he had 'made a man of him', and whom he was wont to invite to eat macaroni at his own table. This puss got knighted, and rejoiced in the name of Sir John Langbourne. In his early days he was a frisky, inconsiderate, and, to say the truth, somewhat profligate gentleman, and had, according to the report of his patron, the habit of seducing light and giddy young ladies, of his own race, into the gardens of Queen's Square Place: but tired at last, like Soloman, of the pleasures and vanities, he became sedate and thoughtful – took to the church, laid down his knightly title, and was installed as the Reverend John Langbourne. He gradually obtained a great reputation for sanctity and learning, and a Doctor's degree was conferred upon him. When I knew him, in his declining days, he bore no other name than the Reverend Doctor John Langbourne: and he was alike conspicuous for his gravity and philosophy. Great respect was invariably shown his reverence; and it was supposed that he was not far off from a mitre, when old age inter-fered with his hopes and honours. He departed amidst the regrets of his many friends, and was gathered to his fathers, and to eternal rest, in a cemetery in Milton's garden.

🐾 *Sir John Bowring*, 'Autobiographical Recollections', 1887.

Witnesses were called in the suit brought to break the will of Gen. Thomas T. Eckert. Joseph Finn, a carpenter, gave a description of the catnip bed which he asserted the general had caused to be built as his Elberon home for 'Honeybubbles' his cat. According to the carpenter it was a miniature greenhouse. When the family was in New York, he said, it was customary to have catnip shipped there daily.

Bessie Tracey, a servant, was asked about the cat.

'The cat came to the table for every meal,' she said. 'He had a chair like the rest of the family, and the same food that the family ate was served to him. During meals he would walk all over the table and eat the flowers.'

'Would he eat food from other plates than his own?' Justice Greenbaum inquired.

'No. Only from his own plate.'

James Clendennin Eckert, Jr., told of a quarrel between Mr and Mrs Thomas Eckert . . .
'Was Honeybubbles the cat at the table when you dined with our grandfather?' Mr Palmer asked.

'He was always there. One day he began clawing and I asked grandpa "Do you want the cat to do that?" and he answered: "No. Put the cat out." He asked me if the cat annoyed me, and I replied: "No, as long as he doesn't souse his tail in my coffee." He told me not to speak of my dislike for Honeybubbles before my uncle.'

Joanna M Eckert, the nineteen year old daughter of James Clendennin Eckert, took the stand.

'Have you seen this before?' asked lawyer Nicoll, holding up a piece of bric-a-brac with a small card attached.

Miss Eckert identified it as something her grandfather had shown her on his birthday, April 23, 1910.

'He told me it was a gift from Honeybubbles, the cat,' she added.

The testimony of Thomas C Ennever, the lawyer who drew Gen. Eckert's will . . . 'Gen. Eckert was seated at one end of the table and Tom at the other end. The other guests were Miss Eagan, Mr and Mrs Page and Miss Page – and big black cat. Before luncheon Gen. Eckert had asked me if I minded sitting at the table with a cat, and I told him I didn't.'

🐾 *The New York Times* reports of a court case in 1914

Poor Mrs Herbert told me that her chief comfort was in a little Chinese Dog of his, which he was not very fond of either (he always said he liked Christians better than beasts, but which used to come and kiss her eyelids and lick the tears from her cheeks. I remember thinking this childish. But now I don't. My cat does just the same to me. Dumb beasts observe you so much more than talking beings; and know so much better what you are thinking of.

🐾 *Florence Nightingale*, Letter to her mother, 1862

Chapter Seven

Remarkable Cats

Cats really seem to vary in their temperament as
much as human beings. There are refined cats, who
find their proper sphere in the drawing room; there
are boorish cats who are out of their element when
removed from the kitchen or cellar; there are robber
cats . . . carrying on an open system of marauding;
and there are trickish cats, who cheat their companions of their dinners. In fine, there is hardly a trait of
human character, which does not find its representa-
tion in one of these animals. Some cats appear to
have a strong sense of humour, and will resist almost
every temptation when they are placed in trust. Still,
some temptations appear to be so powerful that the
honourable feelings cannot resist them. For example,
Minnie will resist every lure except a piece of fried
sole; and Pret could never withstand the allurements
of a little jug of milk or bottled stout. That the palate

of a cat should be pleased with milk is natural
enough, be the milk in jug or saucer; but that bottled
stout should delight the animal appears passing
strange . . .

🐾 **Rev. John Wood**, 'The Illustrated Natural
History', 1874

Last year I took a little cat with me on a bicycle tour.
It sat in a basket on the handle bars, and appeared to
enjoy everything except 'coasting'. Like Gunga Din it
'didn't seem to know the use of fear' and its composure
was never ruffled. It went down the Wye in a boat, it
travelled by rail and in carts or buses. It went through
its ablutions on the crowded platform of Bristol
Station with the utmost nonchalance. It went for long
country walks, following like a dog, and jumping
carefully over the puddles, and delicately avoiding wet
places. If a cart came along it would spring into the
bushes at the side of the road and sit like Brer Rabbit
in the briar patch, with just its head sticking out. A
very pleasant feature of William's tour was the warm

welcome he received from everyone whose hospitality he enjoyed. Rather to my surprise the innkeepers at the places where we stopped, far from objecting to such a strange travelling companion, without exception, made quite a fuss about him, and petted and admired him to an extent which should have turned his head.

William is now too heavy to go out cycling but he still goes for walks when we can take him with us without risk of meeting strange dogs. His extreme fearlessness increases the danger as I very much doubt if he would realise that there could be any necessity for defending himself.

Lady Julia Chance, 'A Book of Cats', 1898

Montague Michael
You're much too fat,
You wicked old, wily old,
Well-fed cat.

All night you sleep
On a cushion of silk,
And twice a day
I bring you milk.

And once in a while
When you catch a mouse,
You're the proudest person
In all the house.

🐾 *Anonymous*

Christina (Rossetti, the poet and the writer's sister) left
me another small legacy in the furry form of a cat. While
very fond of animals of most sorts, she was not particularly addicted to the keeping and fondling of 'pets'; but
she had a dark semi-Persian female cat, Muff, which

had been with her for some years . . . Muff remained with me until her death near the end of 1898: a highly prolific puss, who must, I presume, have given birth altogether to something like a hundred kittens. As soon as a brood was near at hand, she would retire into the safe seclusion of a cupboard or drawer. Her insatiable appetite for milk was surprising: no milk jug or other vessel was sacred from her instant and undisguised irruption. If I wanted to get some milk in my tea or coffee while Muff was in the room, I had to pour it *instanter* from jug to cup, or Muff's nose inside the jug would have forestalled me. She would jump from the floor on to my shoulder, and stolidly abide there as long as permitted; would follow me upstairs step by step, rubbing her head against my ankles, and half tripping me up; and would sit for hours on my writing table as I wrote. The amount of pleasure which I got out of this cat and her quaint ways was extreme: some of it was clearly due to her association with Christina's memory, but by no means the whole.

🐾 *William Michael Rossetti*, 'Some Reminiscences', 1906

Eckert, an Englishman (was) a person famous for the
number, ingenuity and imposing magnitude of his lies
. . . All of a sudden Eckert said:

'Oh by the way! I came near forgetting. I have got
a thing here to astonish you. Such a thing as neither
you nor any other man ever heard of – I've got a cat
that will eat cocoanut! Common green cocoanut –
and not only eat the meat, but drink the milk. It is so
– I'll swear to it.' . . .

He went in the house. Bascom said:

'There – what did I tell you? . . . Cat eat a cocoanut
– oh, my! Now that is just his way, exactly – he will tell
the absurdest lie, and trust to luck to get out of it
again. Cat eat a cocoanut – the innocent fool!'

Eckert approached with his cat, sure enough.

Bascom smiled. Said he:

'I'll hold the cat – you bring the cocoanut.'

Eckert split one open, and chopped up some
pieces. Bascom smuggled a wink to me, and proffered
a slice of the fruit to puss. She snatched it, swallowed
it ravenously, and asked for more!

🐾 **Mark Twain** (Samuel Langhorne Clemens),
'Roughing It', 1872

Eponine attached herself particularly to me . . . She comes running up when she hears the front door bell, receives the visitors, conducts them to the drawing room, talks to them – yes, talks to them – with little chirruping sounds, that do not in the least resemble the language cats use in talking to their own kind, but which simulate the articulate speech of man . . . Then when I come in she discreetly retires to an armchair or a corner of the piano, like a well bred animal who knows what is correct in good society. Pretty little Eponine gave so many proofs of intelligence, good disposition and sociability, that by common consent she was raised to the dignity of a *person* . . . This dignity conferred on her the privilege of eating at table like a person instead of out of a saucer in the corner of the room like an animal.

So Eponine had a chair next to me at breakfast and dinner, but on account of her small size she was allowed to rest her two front paws on the edge of the table. Her place was laid without spoon or fork, but she had her glass. She went right through the dinner dish by dish, from soup to dessert, waiting for her turn to be helped, and behaving with such propriety and nice manners as one would like to see in many children. She made her appearance at the first sound of the bell, and on going into the dining-room one found her already in her place, sitting up in her chair with her paws resting on the edge of the tablecloth, and seeming to offer you her little face to kiss, like a well-brought-up little girl who is affectionately polite towards her parents and elders. As one finds flaws in diamonds, spots on the sun, and shadows on perfection itself, so Eponine, it must be confessed, had a passion for fish . . . She became nearly frantic over fish, and, like a child who is filled with the expectation of dessert, she sometimes rebelled at her soup when she knew (from previous investigations in the kitchen) that fish was coming. When this happened she was not helped, and I would say to her coldly: 'Mademoiselle, a person who is not hungry for soup cannot be hungry for fish,' and the dish would be pitilessly carried away from under her nose. Convinced that matters were serious, greedy Eponine would swallow her soup in all haste, down to the last drop, polishing off the last crumb of bread or bit of macaroni, and would then turn round and look at me with pride, like someone who has conscientiously done his duty. She was then given her portion, which she consumed with great satisfaction . . .

🐾 *Theophile Gautier*, 'A Domestic Menagerie', 1899

When Cambyses invested Pelusium, as being the entrance to Egypt, the Egyptians with great resolution defended it, advancing formidable machines against the besiegers and from the catapults throwing darts, stones and fire. Cambyses ranged before his front line dogs, sheep, cats, ibises, and whatever animals the Egyptians hold sacred. The fear of hurting the animals, which they regard with veneration, instantly checked their operations. Cambyses took Pelusium and thus opened himself a passage into Egypt.

🐾 *Polyaenus the Macedonian*, 'Stratagems of War', c. AD 162

My grandmother's cat, after living a blameless life for upwards of eleven years, took to drink in her old age and was run over while in a state of intoxication (oh, the justice of it!) by a brewer's dray . . .

A leaky beer-tap was the cause of her downfall. A saucer used to be placed underneath to catch the drippings. One day the cat, coming in thirsty and finding nothing else to drink, lapped up a little, liked it, and lapped a little more, went away for half an hour, and came back and finished the saucerful – then sat down beside it and waited for it to fill up again.

From that day till the hour she died, I don't think that cat was ever once sober. Her days she passed in a drunken stupor before the kitchen fire. Her nights she spent in the beer cellar.

My grandmother, shocked and grieved beyond expression, gave up her beer barrel and adopted bottles. The cat, thus condemned to enforced abstinence, meandered about the house for a day and half in a disconsolate, quarrelsome mood. Then she disappeared, returning at eleven o'clock as tight as a drum.

Where she went, and how she managed to procure the drink, we never discovered; but the same programme was repeated every day. Some time during the morning she would contrive to elude our vigilance and escape; and late every evening she would come reeling home across the fields in a condition that I will not sully my pen by attempting to describe. It was on a Saturday night that she met the sad end to which I have before alluded. She must have been very drunk, for the man told us that, because of the darkness and because his horses were tired, he was proceeding at little more than a snail's pace.

🐾 *Jerome K Jerome* (1859–1927), author and humourist

My cat has taken to mulled port and rum punch. Poor old dear! He is all the better for it. Dr W. B. Richardson says that the lower animals always refuse alcoholic drinks, and gives that as a reason why humans should do so too. A very pretty reason, is it not?

🐾 *Eliza Savage*, Letter to Samuel Butler, 1879

The Arabian served for the remainder of his life in the same stud, producing a yearly succession of prodigies of the species. He died in 1753, in his twenty-ninth year, and his remains were deposited in a covered passage leading to the stable, a flat and thankless stone, bare of any inscription, being placed over him. The mutual attachment of animals of a different genus, when placed in a state of society, has often been remarked. Thus there was a reciprocal affection, of many years standing, between the Godolphin Arabian and a black cat, and a portrait of the cat was taken with that of the horse. Poor puss would not long survive her friend. She placed herself, seemingly in a mournful attitude, upon his dead carcase, where she remained fixed until it was removed from the building, then followed it to the place of burial under the gateway near the running stable, sat upon it whilst it continued above ground, and afterwards crawled slowly and reluctantly away, and was never seen again, until her dead body was found in the hayloft.

🐾 *John Lawrence*, 'The History of Delineation of the Horse', 1809

September 5th – Thence homeward having passed through Cheapside and Newgate Market, all burned (in the Fire of London, 1666) . . . I did also see a poor cat taken out of a hole in a chimney, joining the wall of the Exchange, with the hair all burned off its body and yet alive.

🐾 **Samuel Pepys** *(1633–1703)*, diarist and civil servant

You, who've rejected the pick of the dish
And flatly refuse to be stirred
By the mention of meat, if you know there is fish,
Or of fish, if you know there is bird,
Who insist on your sole being *a la bonne femme*,
And your chicken direct from the breast,
Who will only touch trout that has recently come
From the shadowy shoals of the Test,
You who drink nothing that isn't Grade A
And would turn up your nose at a mouse,
Whom I've actually seen moving coldly away
From an underhung portion of grouse,
You who will listlessly trifle and toy

With a dream of a cod kedgeree,
Are eating with every appearance of joy
A very decayed bumble bee.

🐾 *Anonymous*

During the Crimean War, Colonel Stuart Wortley's cat
visited the doctor's tent to get a bayonet wound in the
foot examined and bandaged. She was found by the
colonel wounded after the capture of the Malakoff, and
was by him taken daily for a time to the regimental
surgeon to have the wound dressed. But when he
became himself ill, and unable to take her as usual, she
went herself, and 'sat quietly down for her foot to be
examined, and have its usual bandaging.'

🐾 *William Lauder Lindsay*, 'Mind in the
   Lower Animals', 1879

On Monday, September 9, 1940, she endured horrors and perils beyond the power of words to tell.

Shielding her kitten in a sort of recess in the house (a spot she selected only three days before the tragedies occurred), she sat the whole frightful night of bombing and fire, guarding her little kitten.

The roofs and masonry exploded, the whole house blazed, four floors fell through in front of her. Fire and ruin all around her.

Yet she stayed calm and steadfast and waited for help.

We rescued her in the early morning while the place was still burning, and by the mercy of Almighty God she and her kitten were not only saved, but unhurt.

Inscription in a City of London church, now removed.

Pangur, my white cat, and I,
We each a different skill apply;
His art is all in hunting mice,
Mine is in thought, deep and precise.

My greatest joy is just to sit
And con my page with subtle wit;
While Pangur Ban will frisk and play
Nor envy me my quieter way.

We are companions, never bored
In our small house, in true accord
We test our faculties, and find
Some occupation for the mind.

He, by his arts, can trap and kill
A hapless mouse with perfect skill.
And I, after much careful gleaning
Can bring to light a hidden meaning.

His eye, as keen as any sword,
Is focussed on the skirting board;
While I direct my milder looks
Upon the knowledge in my books.

When he pursues a mouse with speed,
Pangur rejoices in the deed;
I exult when in the brain
Some knotty point at last comes plain.

Though we are always thus together,
We neither one obstruct the other;
Pangur and I pursue alone
Two separate arts, to each his own.

His curious work is his delight,
Which he rehearses day and night;
And daily I bring clarity
Where there had been obscurity.

🐾 *Unknown Irish monk*, eighth century

At sea I was lucky enough to command three
destroyers – and survive – between 1941 and 1949,
no doubt due to the presence aboard of my personal
kittens. A black cat is always good luck. They all
came from my home in Keswick, where Tess, a

tabby delighted our daughter with a succession of families. In HMS Verdun there was black-and-white Whisky who helped me escort many East Coast convoys. He, and my later cats, spent time mainly in my cabin or in the wardroom and there were little trays of sand strategically placed near my cabin for them. They slept on my bunk generally. Whisky distinguished himself by falling overboard in Rosyth harbour, and one of my crew, a noble fellow, jumped in to the rescue. On one occasion a German airman whom we had picked up after shooting down his aircraft, was put in my cabin for safe custody, but Whisky very rightly refused to talk to him.

Georgie, a black female, served with me in the brand new destroyer, HMS Ulster, which I skippered from June 1943 to October 1944 in home waters and the Mediterranean. She used to play ping pong in the wardroom. In March 1944 I suspected Georgie had got wed in Naples, where we were escorting convoys, bombarding enemy positions near Anzio and helping to sink the German submarine U223. I signalled that fact to another destroyer,

adding 'the honeymoon will be spent in Capri . . . ',
but error crept in, and the kittens did not arrive till
much later. We had returned to the UK for D-Day.
Georgie's kittens, all four black, arrived on my bunk
when we were in Cardiff for repairs. Well, you
know what Welsh cats are! One was retained aboard
and the others distributed to friends. Georgie stayed
in the ship when I left, survived the war and
finished up in Australia.

My third sea cat was another black female named
Poppet. She joined a brand new destroyer, HMS
Concord at Portsmouth in March 1947. We sailed
shortly after for China Station. I had a very nice
cabin on upper deck, next to the wardroom, and
Poppet just swanned around on the upper deck. As
we were crossing the Indian ocean, I remember
watching with agony from the bridge as Poppet sat
right forward, outside the guard rails, watching the
bow wave and saying gently with the ship's motion.
But her balance was perfect and all was well.

We were alongside at Hong Kong for Christmas
1947, and one night Poppet broke ship, much to my
distress. I was broken hearted at the thought of her

wandering around the dockyard. The Chinese then sometimes ate cats. She disappeared for four days but turned up again and returned safely back on board before we sailed for Japan. She produced four black kittens in my bunk in Yokohama. In due course the youngsters were drafted to other destroyers and friends in Hong Kong. I always think Poppet's effort, born in Keswick, Wed in Hong Kong and a mother of kittens in Yokohama was noteworthy.

🐾 **Commander William Donald**
(1910–2002), Letter

Thou hast seen Atossa sage
Sit for hours beside thy cage;
Thou wouldst chirp, thou foolish bird,
Flutter chirp – she never stirred!
What were now these toys to her?
Down she sank amid her fur;
Eyed thee with a soul resigned –
And thou deemedst cats were kind!

Cruel, but composed and bland,
Dumb, inscrutable and grand,
So Tiberius might have said
Had Tiberius been a cat.

🐾 *Matthew Arnold* (1822–1888), poet

I can never speak of cats without a sentiment of regret for my poor Trim, the favourite of all our ships' company on the *Spyall*. This good natured purring animal was born on board His Majesty's ship the *Roundabout* in 1799 during a passage from the Cape of Good Hope to Botany Bay . . . In playing with his little brothers and sisters upon deck by moonlight, when the ship was lying tranquilly in harbour, the energy and elasticity of his movements sometimes carried him so far beyond his mark that he fell over-board: but this was far from being a misfortune; he learned to swim and to have no dread of water; and when a rope was thrown over to him, he took hold of it like a man, and ran up it like a cat. In a short time he was able to mount up the gangway steps quicker

than his master, or even than the first lieutenant . . .
His desire to gain a competent knowledge in practical
seamanship was not less than he showed for experi-
mental philosophy. The replacing of a topmast carried
away, or taking a reef in the sails, were what most
attracted his attention at sea; and at all times, when
there was more bustle upon deck than usual, he never
failed to be present and in the midst of it; for as I
have before hinted, he was endowed with an unusual
degree of confidence and courage, and having never
received anything but good from men, he believed all
to be his friends, and he was the friend of all. When
the nature of the bustle upon deck was not understood
by him, he would mew and rub his back up against
the legs or one and the other, frequently at the risk of
being trampled under foot, until he obtained the
attention of someone to satisfy him, He knew what
good discipline required, and on taking in a reef, never
presumed to go aloft until the order was issued; but so
soon as the officer had given the words 'Away up
aloft!', up he jumped along with the seamen; and so
active and zealous was he that none could reach the
top before or so soon as he did. His zeal, however,

never carried him beyond a sense of dignity: he did not lay out on the yard like a common seaman. But always remained seated upon the cap, to inspect like an officer. This assumption of authority to which, it must be confessed, his rank, though great as a quadruped, did not entitle him amongst men, created no jealousy; for he always found some good friend ready to caress him after the business was done, and to take him down in his arms . . .

Trim was admitted upon the table of almost every officer and man in the ship: in the gunroom he was always the first ready for dinner, but though he was commonly seated a quarter of an hour before any other person, his modest reserve was such that his voice was not heard until everybody else was served. He then put in his request, not for a full allowance – he was too modest – nor did he desire there should be laid for him a plate, knife, fork or spoon, with all which he could very well dispense, but by a gentle caressing mew he petitioned for a little, little bit, a kind of tythe from the plate of each.; and it was to no purpose to refuse it, for Trim was enterprising in time of need, as he was gentle and well bred in ordinary times. Without the greatest attention to each morsel, in the person whom he had petitioned in vain, he would ship it off the fork with his paw, on its passage to the mouth, with such dexterity and air so graceful that it rather excited admiration than anger.

🐾 *Matthew Flinders* *(1774–1814)*, 'Trim'

Among the weapons and artworks at the National Army Museum, Chelsea, in a quite corner on the first floor, there squats one of the too-often-missed stars: Crimea Tom, survivor of the siege of Sebastapol . . . When Russia's leading naval base in the Black Sea fell on September 9th, 1855, the British and French forces found death and confusion everywhere. But amid the rubble was Tom, a little thin on it but clearly a born winner.

Captain William Gair of the 16th Dragoon Guards, took charge and carefully fed and groomed him back to his old self. Tom was particularly lucky since Captain Gair held a high post in the commissary, which the cat soon discovered looked after the army's food supplies.

In the painting Tom rests on a box, placed centrally, and quietly ponders life's ups and downs.

:paw: *James Dowsing*, 'The London Cat', 1997

In the great Zoological gardens of Marseilles we found specimens of all the animals the world produces, I think . . . The boon companion of the colossal elephant was a common cat! This cat had a fashion of climbing up the elephants' hind legs, and roosting on his back. She would sit up there, with her paws curved under her breast, and sleep in the sun half the afternoon. It used to annoy the elephant at first and he would reach up and take her down, but she would go aft and climb up again. She persisted until she finally conquered the elephant's prejudices, and now they are inseparable friends. The cat plays about her comrade's fore feet or his trunk often, until dogs approach, and then she goes aloft out of danger. The elephant has annihilated several dogs lately, that pressed his companion too closely.

:paw: *Mark Twain* (Samuel Langhorne Clemens) (1835–1910), novelist

A very pretty and effective exercise for a cat is hoop-leaping. It costs little trouble to teach and every cat will learn it. For this you must be provided with a little switch, not to hit the cat, but merely to make a noise in the air. Pronounce the word hoop each time you hold the article in front of her, and she will soon learn to go through it in whatever position you hold it. Or you may have a series of hoops, at different elevations, placed in the garden a few yards apart; or, better still, hung from the couples of a barn or grain-loft. On these last a young and healthy cat soon becomes quite a wonderful performer; and, if you wish her to be still more highly educated in the hoop business, you can dip your hoop in metholated spirits of wine and set fire to it; she will go through just the same. Or cover the hoop with thin tissue paper and teach her to go through it. At first the paper must be oiled so as to be nearly transparent. A friend of mine, coming home at twelve o'clock, heard an awful noise and rattling in an outhouse, which he had fitted up as a cat gymnasium. On going in with a light he was surprised to find two full grown kittens performing – they had been giving a dark seance on their own account.

🐾 *Gordon Stables*, 'Cats', 1876

Mr Crowder, one of the proprietors of (Lusby's Music) Hall possessed a favourite tabby and tortoise-shell cat, which was well known to the frequenters of the hall. The cat had a family of four kittens, which she was allowed to keep in a basket at the rear of the stage. Soon after the fire was discovered, the cat was seen rushing about frantically. She several times attempted to make her way down the corridor in the direction of the stage, but each time was beaten back by the smoke. Presently she reappeared with one of the kittens in her mouth. This she laid carefully down at her master's feet in the small hall, which the fire had not touched. Again she rushed through the smoke, and again reappeared with a kitten, and this manoeuvre she repeated the third time.

She was now apparently half-blinded and choked by the smoke she had passed through, and it was thought she would be content; but she seemed unable to rest while she knew that one of her kittens was still in danger; and giving a look at the little strug-gling group on the floor, the cat, evading someone who tried to stop her, once more dashed down the corridor towards the seething mass of flames which by this time had enveloped the stage and the lower end of the hall. Her return was anxiously awaited, but she did not come back. Afterwards, when examining the ruins, some of the firemen came across the charred and blackened remains of the mother and kitten, lying side by side where the fire had overtaken them.

🐾 *Anonymous*, 'The Animal World', 1887

A very remarkable accident befell Henry Wriothesly, Earl of Southampton, the friend and companion of the Earl of Essex, in his fatal insurrection: after he had been confined here (in the Tower of London) for a short time, he was surprised by a visit from his favourite cat, which had found its way to the Tower, and, as tradition says, reached its master by descending the chimney of his apartment. I have seen – an original portrait of this Earl, in the place of his confinement in a black dress and cloak, with the faithful animal sitting by him.

🐾 *Thomas Pennant*, 'Some Account of London', 1813

Gertie, long-haired and black and white, is a luvvy. Her whole life is the theatre – in particular the Phoenix Theatre, London, and the Musical Blood Brothers by Willy Russell, which has been playing ever since she arrived there from the Cats Protection League three years ago.

'Gertie never comes on stage when the play's on,' says Rikki Newman, the Phoenix Theatre's master carpenter, who looks after her. 'She's far too well behaved – a true professional.

'She knows the music for the interval – that is when she is fed. And she also knows the music at the end, for she is lining up then to go on to the stage, which is the warmest part of the theatre.'

Gertie is named after Gertrude Lawrence. Her territory is backstage, the understage and the high fly floor. 'We didn't know she could get up there till she appeared one day when we were working there,' says Newman.

Cats are a theatre tradition; the obituary of Gertie's predecessor, Tabs, appeared in the Stage. Gertie is just as dedicated as Tabs, says Newman. 'She has no interest in the world outside the theatre.'

🐾 *Celia Haddon*, 1997.

The day being arrived on which Mr Lunardi had informed the public that he would ascend with the Air Balloon, at a very early hour of the day about a hundred and fifty thousand spectators assembled. The machine mounted with slow and gradual majesty into the air. Mr Lunardi was accompanied in his aerial passage by a couple of pigeons, a cat, and a favourite lap dog. In about a quarter of an hour, sailing over Pall Mall at an immense height, he met with a counter current of air, which carried him rapidly a north easterly course, over Highgate. When Mr Lunardi had gained the utmost altitude of his ascension, he felt so strong a propensity for sleeping, that it was with the utmost difficulty he could keep himself awake; the cold at this time became so intensely piercing, as to render Mr Lunardi's situation in it almost unsupportable. The cat was benumbed and had not Mr Lunardi's regard for his dog led him to afford him the warmth of his bosom, the animal would inevitably have perished. After Mr Lunardi had been up about an hour and a half, the thermometer stood at 35 degrees, when the atmosphere was so cold, that icicles were upon his clothes and he was fearful that his balloon would burst; at this time he drank several glasses of wine. On throwing out some air the thermometer rose to 50, when the atmosphere was delightful. At Northaw he threw out his cat, which was taken up alive.

Anonymous, 'Lunardi's Grand Aerostatic Voyage Through the Air', 1784

Moses Pitt . . . narrates the case of Mr. Morgan, a surgeon of Liverpool, who, being put in prison there, was ultimately reduced so low by poverty, neglect, and hunger, as to catch by a cat mice for his sustenance.

Robert Chambers, 'The Book of Days', 1864

Chapter Eight

Farewell

Who can believe that there is no soul behind those luminous eyes!

🐾 *Theophile Gautier* *(1811–1872)*, writer

I want him to have another living summer,
to lie in the sun and enjoy the *douceur de vivre* –
because the sun, like golden rum in a rummer,
is what makes an idle cat *un tout petit peu ivre* –

I want him to lie stretched out, contented,
revelling in the heat, his fur all dry and warm,
an Old Age Pensioner, retired, resented,
by no one, and happinesses in a beelike swarm

to settle on him – postponed for another season
that last fated hateful journey to the vet
from which there is no return (and age the reason),
which soon must come – as I cannot forget.

🐾 *Gavin Ewart* (1916–1995), 'A 14-Year-Old
   Convalescent Cat in the Winter'

Our cat was raptured up to heaven. He'd never liked
heights, so he tried to sink his claws into whatever
invisible snake, giant hand, or eagle was causing him
to rise in this manner, but he had no luck.

When he got to heaven, it was a large field. There
were lots of little pink things running around that he
thought at first were mice. Then he saw God sitting
in a tree. Angels were flying here and there with their
fluttering white wings; they were making sounds like
doves. Every once in a while God would reach out
with its large furry paw and snatch one of them out
of the air and crunch it up. The ground under the
tree was littered with bitten-off angel wings.

Our cat went politely over to the tree.

Meow, said our cat.

Meow, said God. Actually it was more like a roar.

I always thought you were a cat, said our cat, but I wasn't sure.

In heaven all things are revealed, said God. This is the form in which I choose to appear to you.

I'm glad you aren't a dog, said our cat. Do you think I could have my testicles back?

Of course, said God. They're over behind that bush.

Our cat had always known his testicles must be somewhere. One day he'd woken up from a fairly bad dream and found them gone. He'd looked everywhere for them – under sofas, under beds, inside closets – and all the time they were here, in heaven! He went over to the bush, and, sure enough, there they were. They reattached themselves immediately.

Our cat was very pleased. Thank you, he said to God.

God was washing its elegant long whiskers. De rien, said God.

Would it be possible for me to help you catch some of those angels? said our cat.

You never liked heights, said God, stretching itself

out along the branch, in the sunlight. I forgot to say there was sunlight.

True, said our cat. I never did. There were a few disconcerting episodes he preferred to forget. Well, how about some of those mice?

They aren't mice, said God. But catch as many as you like. Don't kill them right away. Make them suffer.

You mean, play with them? said our cat. I used to get in trouble for that.

It's a question of semantics, said God. You won't get in trouble for that here.

Our cat chose to ignore this remark, as he did not know what 'semantics' was. He did not intend to make a fool of himself. If they aren't mice, what are they? he said. Already he'd pounced on one. He held it down under his paw. It was kicking, and uttering tiny shrieks.

They're the souls of human beings who have been bad on Earth, said God, half-closing its yellow-green eyes. Now if you don't mind, it's time for my nap.

What are they doing in heaven then? said our cat.

Our heaven is their hell, said God. I like a balanced universe.

🐾 *Margaret Atwood*, 'The Tent', 2006

274

Ye rats, in triumph elevant your ears!
Exult, ye mice! – for Fate's aborred shears
Of Dick's nine lives have slit the catguts nine
Henceforth he mews 'midst choirs of cats divine! . . .
Calumnious cats, who circulate *faux pas*,
And reputations maul with murderous claws;
Shrill cats, whom fierce domestic brawls delight,
Cross cats, who nothing want but teeth to bite;
Starch cats of puritanic aspect sad,
And learned cats, who talk their husbands mad;
Confounded cats, who cough, and croak, and cry,
And maudlin cats who drink eternally;
Fastidious cats, who pine for costly cates,
And jealous cats who catechize their mates;
Cat prudes who, when they're asked the question,
  squall,
And ne'er give answer categorical;
Uncleanly cats, who never pare their nails,
Cat gossips, full of Canterbury tales;
Cat-grandams, vexed with asthmas and catarrhs,
And superstitious cats, who curse their stars;
Cats of each class, craft, calling, and degree,
Mourn Dick's calamitous catastrophe.

Though no funereal cypress shade thy tomb,
For thee the wreaths of Paradise shall bloom;
There, while Grimalkin's mew her Richard greets,
A thousand cats shall purr on purple seats . . .
There shall the worthies of the whiskered race
Elysian mice o'er floors of sapphire chase,
Midst beds or aromatic marum stray,
Or raptured rove beside the milky way.
Kittens, than eastern houris fairer seen,
Whose bright eyes glisten with immortal green,
Shall smooth for tabby swains their yielding fur,
And to their amorous mews, assenting purr . . .

🐾 *George Huddesford* (1749–1809), 'Monody
on the Death of Dick an Academical Cat'

We often mourn and weep for the loss of those beasts
we love, so do they many times for the loss of us.

🐾 *Michel Montaigne*, 'Essays', 1580

In Rue Mansard, I had a cat named Mime after a character in the Walkyrie. Mime was beautiful as love. He was a superb black tom cat, but he gave off a formidable odour and would not stop scratching my curtains. I was forced to hand him over to a man skilled in the art who brought him back to us in a condition of utter neuterdom. From that day onwards, Mime plunged into a sadness blacker than his coat. We live on the fifth floor. Mime had been accustomed, at certain moments of the day, to make a tour of the zinc-covered cornice along the façade under our windows. One morning, I saw him – or I believed I saw him – deliberately hurl himself into the street from that cornice. The impact of his fall from such a height completely shattered his body. I swear to you that I felt convinced that Mime had committed suicide.

🐾 *Catulle Mendez* *(1841–1910)*, poet and writer

How fickle's health! When sickness thus
So sharp, so sudden visits Puss!
A warning fair, and instance good,
To show how frail are flesh and blood,
That Fate has mortals at a call,
Men, women, children – cats and all . . .

Now joyful mice, skip, frisk and play,
And safely revel, night and day.
The garrets, kitchens, stairs and entry,
Unguarded by that dreadful sentry.

The pantry now is open set,
No fear for puss therein to get,
With chicken sold to run away,
Or sip the cream set by for tea . . .

Though I have heard a saying that
Some three times three lives has a cat;
Should Death then now the conquest gain,
And feeble Bob, with struggle vain,
To his resistless fate give way,
Yet come to life another day,

How will Time scratch his old bald pate,
To see himself so Bobbed, so bit,
To find that Bob has eight lives more
To lose, e'er he can him secure.
Should he however, this bout die,
What pen should writ his elegy?
No living bard is fit, not one;
Since Addison and Parnel's gone;
Or such another pen, as that
Which wrote so fine on Montaigne's cat.

🐾 *John Winstanley* (1678–1751), 'Upon a
   Friends Pet Cat, Being Sick'

The last time I saw Persis was once when she came to
greet me at the door, and lifting her I noticed how
light she was; and again I saw her coming downstairs
on some business of her own, with an air at once
furtive and arrogant, quaint in so small a creature. Then
Persis vanished. She had been absent before for days at
a time; had once disappeared for three weeks and
returned thin and exhausted. So at first we did not

trouble; then we called her in the garden, in the fields and the coverts, wrote to find out if she had returned to some old home, and offered a reward for her finding; but all was fruitless. I do not know now whether she had gone away as some creatures do, to die alone, for the signs of age were on her; or if she had met a speedy death at the hands of a gamekeeper while she was following up some wild romance of the woods.

So vanished secretly from life that strange troubled little soul of a cat – a troubled soul, for it was not the animal loves and hates which were too much for her – these she had ample spirit and courage to endure, but she knew a jealous love for beings beyond her dim power of comprehension, a passionate desire for praise and admiration from creatures whom she did not understand, and these waked a strange conflict and turmoil in the vivid and limited nature, troubling her relations with her kind, filling her now with black despairs, and painful passions, and now with serene, half understood content. Who shall know whether a creature like this can ever utterly perish? How shall we who know so little of their nature profess to know so much of their future?

🐾 **Margaret Benson**, 'The Soul of a Cat', 1909

By Rome's dim relics there walks a man,
Eyes bent; and he carries a basket and spade;
I guess what impels him to scrape and scan;
Yea, his dreams of that Empire long decayed.

'Vast was Rome,' he must muse, 'in the world's
   regard,
Vast it looms there still, vast it ever will be,'
And he stoops as to dig and unmine some shard
Left there by those who are held in such memory.

But no; in his basket, see, he has brought
A little white furred thing, stiff of limb,
Whose life never won from the world a thought;
It is this, and not Rome, that is moving him.

And to make it a grave he has come to the spot,
And he delves in the ancient dead's long home;
Their fames, their achievements the man knows
   not;
The furred thing is all to him – nothing Rome!

'Here say you that Caesar's warriors lie? –
But my little white cat was my only friend!
Could she but live, might the record die
Of Caesar, his legions, his arms, his end!'

🐾 *Thomas Hardy* *(1840–1928)*, 'The Roman
Gravemounds'

Because of their fear of such a punishment any who
have caught sight of one of these animals (cats) lying
dead retreat to a great distance and shout with lamentations and protestations that they found the animal
already dead. So deeply implanted also in the heart of
the common people is their superstitious love for these
animals and so unalterable are the feelings cherished
by every man regarding the honour due to them, that
once, at the time when the Romans had not yet given
Ptolemy their king the appellation of 'friend' and the
people were trying hard to win the favour of the
embassy from Italy which was then visiting Egypt and,
in their fear, were intent on upon giving no cause for
complaint or war, when one of the Romans killed a

cat and the mob rushed in a crowd to his house,
neither the official sent by the king to beg the man
off nor the fear of Rome which they all felt were
enough to save the man from punishment, even though
his act had been an accident. And this incident we
relate, not from hearsay, but we saw it with our own
eyes when we were visiting Egypt.

🐾 *Diodorus Siculus*, 'Bibliotheca Historica',
50 BC

Here lies old Nut,
In pit-hole put;
Death in his claws has got her:
Her claws had tricks
Of pouncing chicks
And so the farmer shot her.

Now do not sneer
At Pussy here,
Nor scoffingly crow o'er her;
Perhaps had you

Deservings due
You had been shot before her.

Of years fifteen,
Great age I ween –
Age e'en in cats we honour:
And now to grow
So wicked, oh!
This blasts her fame, fie on her!

Ah, had she died
By own fireside,
When wintry rheums reduced her,
Her mistress's tears
Had crowned her years,
Nor knave nor fool abused her.

But cats are frail,
Yea, many a tale
Of foolishness they give us.
Now should we say
'Twere not so, –
Pray would anyone believe us?

So, Puss, farewell.
Thy tale I tell
In verse, the long and short on't.
But who and how,
Tell mine, I trow,
Is matter more important.

🐾 *Isaac Taylor*, 'Epitaph on a Cat', 1813

They were created before Adam. Prior to man they shared and share his lot. They had a right in Paradise. They were gathered with the eight souls into the ark. They had a principal part in God's revelations. By animals God made known the way of Man's salvation. Said the law divine, sin must suffer – death for sin. He caused animals to be nurtured for Sacrifice to reveal this great thing. A Lamb proclaimed the gospel of the future Messiah – a lamb slain. When Jesus was born, it was in the presence of animals. The ox knew his owner in the cave of Bethlehem, and the ass his Master's crib. In the wilderness the Son of Man was among the beasts of the wild. An ass knew her rider when he rode into Jerusalem royally. Beside all this there have been seen by prophets in their visions horses in heaven, from the scenery of Sachariah to the pale steed of Azrael, angel of death, recorded by St John. Who can read all this and doubt but that animals will roam and feed in the New Earth, wherein righteousness will dwell?

🐾 *Rev. Robert Stephen Hawker*, Letter, 1862

Jeremiah. A Burmese Cat 1991–2006.
Neurotic, Needy but Loving.

🐾 *Tombstone in a garden*

She had a name among the children;
But no one loved though someone owned
Her, locked her out of doors at bedtime
And had her kittens duly drowned.

In spring, nevertheless, this cat
Ate blackbirds, thrushes, nightingales,
And birds of bright voice and plume and flight,
As well as scraps from neighbour's pails.

I loathed and hated her for this;
One speckle on a thrush's breast
Was worth a million such; and yet
She lived long, till God gave her rest.

🐾 *Edward Thomas* (1878–1917), 'A Cat'

I know the case of an old gentleman, who was
extremely fond of a very pretty cat he had; and pussy
loved her master dearly. Indeed, cats seem always
particularly partial to the aged. They love to sit beside
them at the fireside, and soothe them with their low,
murmuring song; for they seem to know by instinct
that age is but a second childhood, with only the
grave beyond. The gentleman in question died at an
advanced age. Every one missed and mourned him,
but none so sincerely as pussy. She never sung again,

and nothing could induce her to leave his sitting room. She would sit and gaze for hours at the vacant armchair, as if she couldn't understand why her eyes no longer beheld him she loved. This went on for a fortnight; then one morning poor pussy was found lying stiff and dead on the hearth rug. She had died of grief.

🐾 *Gordon Stables*, 'Friends in Fur', 1876

Ah pity, thines a tender heart
Thy sigh soon heaves thy tears will start
And thou has gen the muse her part
  Salt tears to shed
To mourn and sigh wi sorrows smart
    For pussey dead.

Ah mourning memory neath thy pall
Thou utterst many a piercing call
Pickling in vinegars sour gall
  Ways that are fled
The ways the feats the tricks and all
    Of pussey dead.

Thou tellst of all the gamsome plays
That markt her happy kitten days
– Ah I did love her funney ways
 On the sand floor
But now sad sorrow dampts my lays
    Pusseys no more

Thou paints her flirting round and round
As she was wont wi things she'd found
Chasing the spider oer the ground
 Straws pushing on
Thou paints em on a bosom wound
    Poor pusseys gone

And now poor puss thoust lost thy breath
And desent laid the moulds beneath
As ere a cat coud wish in death
 For their last bed
This to thy memory I bequeath
    Poor pussey dead.

🐾 *John Clare*, 'Sorrows for a Favourite Tabby Cat
who Left This Scene of Troubles Friday Night Nov.
26 1819'

Alas, Grosvenor, this day poor old Rumpel was found dead, after as long and happy a life as cat could wish for, if cats form wishes on that subject. His full titles were: The Most Noble the Archduke Rumpelstiltzchen, Marquis Macbum, Earl Tomlemagne, Baron Raticide, Waowhler, and Skaratch. There should be court mourning in Catland, and if the Dragon (Mr Bedford's cat) wear a black ribbon round his neck, or a band of crape à la militaire round one of the forepaws, it will be but a becoming mark of respect. As we have no catacombs here, he is to be decently interred in the orchard, and cat-mint planted on his grave. Poor creature, it is well that he has thus come to his end after he had become an object of pity. I believe we are each and all, servants included, more sorry for his loss, or rather more affected by it, than anyone of us would like to confess.

🐾 **Robert Southey**, Letter, 1833

Bathsheba! To whom none ever said scat –
No worthier cat
Ever sat on a mat
Or caught a rat.
Requiescat!

🐾 **John Greenleaf Whittier** *(1807–1892),*
'For a Little Girl Mourning her Favourite Cat'

As I look back upon it, Calvin's life seems to me a
fortunate one, for it was natural and unforced. He ate
when he was hungry, slept when he was sleepy, and
enjoyed existence to the very tips of his toes and the
end of his expressive and slow-moving tail. He
delighted to roam about the garden and stroll among
the trees, and to lie on the green grass and luxuriate
in all the sweet influences of summer. You could
never accuse him of idleness, and yet he knew the
secret of repose. The poet who wrote so prettily of
him that his little life was rounded with a sleep
understated his felicity; it was rounded with a good
many. His conscience never seemed to interfere with

his slumbers. In fact, he had good habits and a contented mind. I can see him now walk in at the study door, sit down by my chair, bring his tail artistically about his feet, and look up at me with unspeakable happiness in his handsome face . . .

His departure was as quiet as his advent was mysterious. I only know that he appeared to us in this world in his perfect stature and beauty, and that after a time like Lohengrin, he withdrew. In his illness there was nothing more to be regretted than in all his blameless life . . . It came on gradually, in a kind of listlessness and want of appetite . . . He sat or lay day after day almost motionless . . . His favourite place was on the brightest spot of a Smyrna rug by the conservatory, where the sunlight fell and he could hear the fountain play. If we went to him and exhibited our interest in his condition, he always purred in recognition of our sympathy. And when I spoke his name, he looked up with an expression that said, 'I understand it, old fellow, but it's no use.' He was to all who came to visit him a model of calmness and patience in affliction . . .

One sunny morning he rose from his rug, went into the conservatory (he was very thin then), walked around it deliberately, looking at all the plants he knew, and then went to the bay-window in the dining-room, and stood a long time looking out upon the little field, now brown and sere, and toward the garden, where perhaps the happiest hours of his life had been spent. It was a last look. He turned and walked away, laid himself down upon the bright spot in the rug, and quietly died.

🐾 *Charles Dudley Warner*, 'My Summer in a Garden', 1880

Pet was never mourned as you,
Purrer of the spotless hue,
Plumy tail, and wistful gaze
While you humoured our queer ways,
Or outshrilled your morning call
Up the stairs and through the hall –
Foot suspended in its fall –
While, expectant, you would stand
Arched, to meet the stroking hand;
Till your way you chose to wend
Yonder to your tragic end.

Never another pet for me!
Let your place all vacant be;
Better blankness day by day
Than companion torn away.
Better bid his memory fade,
Better blot each mark he made,
Selfishly escape distress
By contrived forgetfulness,
Than preserve his prints to make
Every morn and eve an ache.

From the chair whereon he sat
Sweep his fur, nor wince thereat;
Rake his little pathways out
Mid the bushes round about;
Smooth away his talons' mark
From the claw-worn pine-tree bark,
Where he climbed as dusk enbrowned
Waiting us who loitered round.

Strange it is this speechless thing,
Subject to our mastering,
Subject for his life and food

To our gift, and time, and mood;
Timid pensioner of us Powers,
His existence ruled by ours,
Should – by crossing at a breath
Into safe and shielded death,
By the merely taking hence
Of his insignificance –
Loom as largened to the sense,
Shape as part, above man's will,
Of the Imperturbable.

As a prisoner, flight debarred,
Exercising in a yard,
Still retain I, troubled, shaken,
Mean estate, by him forsaken;
And this home, which scarcely took
Impress from his little look,
By his faring to the Dim
Grows all eloquent of him.

Housemate, I can think you still
Bounding to the window-sill,
Over which I vaguely see

Your small mound beneath the tree,
Showing in the autumn shade
That you moulder where you played.

🐾 *Thomas Hardy* *(1840–1928)*, 'Last Words To
A Dumb Friend'

Diverse nations, and namely of the most ancient and
noble, have not only received beasts into their society
and company, but allowed them a place far above
themselves; sometimes deeming them to be familiars
and favoured of their Gods, and holding them in a
certain awful respect and reverence more than human
. . . Plutarch . . . saith, that (for example sake) it was
neither the Cat nor the Ox that the Egyptians
adored, but that in those beasts they worshipped
some image of divine faculties . . . The Agrigentines
had an ordinary custom seriously and solemnly to
bury all such beasts as they had held dear; as horses
of rare worth and merit, special dogs, choice or
profitable birds, or such as had but served to make
their children sport. And the sumptuous magnificence

which in all other things was ordinary and peculiar unto them, appeared also most notably in the stately sumptuousness and costly number of monuments erected to that end, which many ages after have endured and been maintained in pride and state. The Egyptians were wont to bury their wolves, their dogs, their cats, their bears, and crocodiles in holy places, embalming their carcasses, and at their deaths to wear mourning weeds for them.

🐾 *Michel Montaigne*, 'Essays', 1580

Strange sickness fell upon this perfect creature
Who walked the equal friend of Man and Nature.
Her little Bodie, e'en as by a shroud,
Lay lapped in its unseen, dishevelling cloud;
Till to her eyes, unmasking but afraid,
The old reply of endless night was made.

🐾 *Frances Cornford* (1886–1960), 'On Maou
   dying at the age of six months'

My dear Lord Aberdare,

I am little able now a days to write albeit I have a great deal of writing to get through.

For, whoever has known me for 30 years has known that for all that time my Cat Foss has been part of my solitary life.

Foss is dead; & I am glad to say did not suffer at all – having become quite paralyzed all on one side of him. So he was placed in a box yesterday & buried deep below the Fig tree at the end of the Orange walk & tomorrow there will be a stone placed giving the date of his death & his age (31 years) – (9 of which 30 were passed in my house.)

> Qui soto è sepolto il mio buon
> Gatto Foxx. Era 30 anni in casa
> Mia, e morì il 26 Novembre
> 1887, di età 31 anni.

(Here lies buried my good Cat Foss. He was 30 years in my house, and died on 26 November 1887, at the age of 31 years.)

All those friends who have known my life will understand that I grieve over this loss. As for myself I am much as usual . . .

At the head of this letter, Lord Aberdare has written
'Last letter from my dear old friend – who died Jan 1888.')

🐾 **Edward Lear**, Letter to Lord Aberdare, 1887

My old cat is dead,
Who would butt me with his head.
He had the sleekest fur.
He had the blackest purr.
Always gentle with us
Was this black puss,
But when I found him today,
Stiff and cold where he lay
His look was a lion's,
Full of rage, defiance:
Oh, he could not pretend
That what came was a friend
But met it in pure hate.
Well died, my old cat.

🐾 **Hal Summers** *(1911–2005)*, 'My Old Cat'

We said goodbye to Tabby last week. She had cancer of the nasal passages and had lost her ability to purr. We went for a last walk in the garden. It was sunny and warm. I had to carry her as she was quite wobbly by this time.

No more will we close our eyes tightly as nose to nose she checks if we are awake in the morning.

No more will she chirrup calling to us on our way out and on our return.

No more will she walk up and down in front of me, if we do not make a move for bed by 11pm. She used to walk to the door whilst looking back to see if we were following.

No more will new ornaments and cut flowers be scrutinised and every new plant, bush or hole in the garden examined.

I still see her everywhere – eating cheese off the grass before the birds had their share or jumping out from her hiding place in the shrubs to give us a fright.

I still feel the warmth of her on my lap as she settles into position. I hope I feel it for some time to come.

🐾 *Elsie Critten*, 'The Death of Tabby', 2001

When cats like him submit to fate,
And seek the Stygian strand,
In silent woe and mimic state
Should mourn the feline band.

For me – full oft at eventide
Enrapt in thought profound,
I hear his solemn footsteps glide
And startle at the sound!

Oft as the murmuring gale draws near
(To fancy's rule consigned),
His tuneful purr salutes my ear,
Soft floating on the wind.

Ann Francis (1738–1800), 'An Elegy on a
Favourite Cat'

They say that most animals, and especially cats, creep away into darkness and solitude to die. He (Nero, a black cat) had been ill for a long time, and in spite of all our care, we knew the end was near, and we dreaded that this instinct might assert itself. But, when the death agony was upon him, and we were looking on, helpless, he crept close to his master, and bore his great pain with patient courage, responding always to the encouragement of his master's voice, and then, having laid for three hours, with his head pillowed in the palm of his master's hand, and the loving, wistful yes fixed immovably upon his face, he died, good and gentle to the last. Do you believe that the spirit was one of those that 'go down into the earth' or that there is no promise of futurity for such love and such intelligence?

🐾 *Anonymous*, The Spectator, 1872

Now Tom's translated, not a mouse
Dare inhabit Heaven's house;
Cherubim shall bring him milk,
Seraphs stroke his coat of silk.

While, with whiskers aureoled,
He shall walk the streets of gold
Or, happily relaxed, lie prone
Deeply purring by the throne.

🐾 *Vivien Bulkley* *(b. 1890)*, 'Cat of Cats'

I must strive to see only God in my friends, and God in my cats.

🐾 *Florence Nightingale* *(1820–1910)*, pioneer of nursing

Have you not observed that when death enters a house, other deaths follow – perhaps my own – and when trouble settles down on a house it multiplies. All our cats except one are dead, and he, poor fellow, follows me about crying and as I fancy nestling about my legs as if he thought we were both lonely and our companions gone.

My path is clear before. Duty done and patience under God's hand and waiting for my time to come also.

 **Robert Stephen Hawker**, Letter, 1863

Acknowledgements

There are copyrights that I could not trace, despite vigorous efforts, in particular the copyright holder of the poem by Vivien Bulkley. The publishers will be happy to rectify any omissions in future editions and I will be happy to pay any fee owing. I would like to thank the following:

The Authors' Licensing and Collecting Society on behalf of Lucy Summers for permission to use 'My Old Cat' by Hal Summers.

Gerard Benson for permission to use 'Duffy' and 'The Scholar's Cat', from *To Catch an Elephant: Poems by Gerard Benson*. Smith/Doorstep 2002, © Gerard Benson.

Curtis Brown Group Ltd for 'Sorrows for a Favourite Tabby Cat who Left This Scene of Troubles Friday Night Nov. 26 1819', by John Clare, from EARLY POEMS OF JOHN CLARE Copyright © Eric Robinson 1989. Reproduced with permission of Curtis Brown Group Ltd, London, on behalf of Eric Robinson.

Curtis Brown Group Ltd for 'Our Cat Enters Heaven', from THE TENT by Margaret Atwood. Copyright ©

London Cat, Its Lives and Times, by James Dowsing. Sunrise Press, 1997, copyright © James Dowsing.

Margo Ewart for 'A 14-Year-Old Convalescent Cat in the Winter', by Gavin Ewart.

Faber and Faber for 'The Ad-dressing of Cats' from *Old Possum's Book of Practical Cats*, by T.S. Eliot, Faber and Faber Ltd, The Estate of T.S. Elliot.

Faber and Faber Ltd for 'Pets' from, *Moon-Bells and Other Poems by Ted Hughes*, Faber and Faber Ltd, 2003, The Estate of Ted Hughes.

Harcourt, USA, for 'The Ad-dressing of Cats' from OLD POSSUM'S BOOK OF PRACTICAL CATS, copyright 1939 by T.S. Eliot, renewed 1967 by Esme Valerie Eliot, reprinted by permission of Harcourt Inc.

HarperCollins, Australia, for an extract from *Trim* by Matthew Flinders, Angus and Robertson and also with thanks to *Overland* magazine, Australia.

Harvard University Press for 'She sights a bird, she chuckles' by Emily Dickinson. Reprinted by permission of the publishers and the Trustees of Amherst College from THE POEMS OF EMILY DICKINSON, Thomas H. Johnson, ed., Cambridge, Mass.: The Belknap Press of Harvard University Press, copyright © 1951, 1955, 1979, 1983 by the President and Fellows of Harvard College.

David Higham Associates for 'The Cat of the House' by Ford Madox Ford.

David Higham Associates for 'Nature Notes: Cats', by

Louis Macneice, from *Collected Poems* edited by E. R. Dodds (Faber & Faber), 1966.

Piet Hein a/s for *Littlecat*. Copyright © Piet Hein Grooks: page 100, LITTLECAT.– Reprinted with kind permission from Piet Hein a/s, DK-5500, Middelfart, Denmark.

Thomas Hinde for permission to quote from *Lewis Carroll. Looking Glass Letters*, published by Collins and Brown.

The Literary Trustees of Walter de la Mare and the Society of Authors as their representative for 'Comfort', 'Double Dutch', and 'Puss' by Walter de la Mare from *The Complete Poems of Walter de la Mare* (1975 reprint).

Jess McAree for permission to use his translation of a passage by Pier Loti, the poem by Hippolyte Taine and the sonnet by François Lemaître.

Hamish McGibbon on behalf of the estate of James McGibbon for permission to use 'Our Office Cat' by Stevie Smith.

New Directions Publishing Corporation, USA, for 'Our Office Cat' by Stevie Smith from *Collected Poems of Stevie Smith*, copyright © 1972 by Stevie Smith. Reprinted by permission of New Directions Publishing Corp.

Ronald Payne for translations of an extract by Timothee Trim (Leo Lespès), *Le Petit Journal*, and one by Catulle Mendez.

Penguin Group for six lines from POEMS FROM THE SANSKRIT, translated with an introduction by John Brough (Penguin Classics, 1968). Copyright © John Brough, 1968.

The Reivers by William Faulkner, published by Chatto and Windus. Reprinted by permission of the Random House Group Ltd.

The Random House Group UK on behalf of Sylvia Townsend for permission to quote from *Sylvia Townsend Warner Letters*, edited by William Maxwell, published by Chatto and Windus. Reprinted by permission of The Random House Group Ltd.

SLL/Sterling Lord Literistic for permission to print the poem 'CAT' by C. Day Lewis. Reprinted by permission of SLL/Sterling Lord Literistic, Inc. Copyright by C. Day Lewis.

Carmelo Lison Tolosana for permission to use the late William Donald's account of cats at sea.

Watson, Little Ltd for permission to quote from EDWARD LEAR: SELECTED LETTERS, edited by Vivien Noakes, Oxford University Press.

A.P. Watt Ltd on behalf of Gráinne Yeats for the poem, THE CAT AND THE MOON, by William Butler Yeats.

Andrea Whittaker for her translation of the poem by Theodor Storm.

Wiley-Blackwell for permission to use 'Connoisseurs' by Dugald S. MacColl, from *Poems*. Basil Blackwell, 1940.